CENTERED LIVING/ CENTERED LEADING:
THE WAY OF LIGHT AND LOVE

The Tao Te Ching Adapted for Christ-Followers

G. Christopher Scruggs

Shiloh Publishing

2009 First Printing

All scriptures not otherwise indicated are from the Holy Bible, New International Version. NIV. Copyright 1973, 1978, 1984. Scripture quotations noted "NLT" or "Message" or other abbreviations noted in the Bibliography are from the New Living Translation, the Message, or other noted translation or paraphrase. Such quotations are used by permission of the publisher and within their guidelines. Each publisher reserves all rights to their translation or paraphrase.

For information regarding permission to reprint material from this book, please mail your request to Shiloh Publishing, 1879 North Germantown Parkway, Cordova, Tennessee 38016 or email Permisio Por Favor at:
permisoporfavor@hotmail.com

Library of Congress in Publication Data
G. Christopher Scruggs 1951-
Centered Living/Centered Leading
The Way of Light and Love
The *Tao Te Ching* adapted for Christ-Followers
Includes bibliographical references

ISBN: 1-4392-4860-5
ISBN-13: 9781439248607
Library of Congress Control Number:2009906667

Published and manufactured in the United States of America
Cover Photo: Kathy T. Scruggs
Photo of Author: Alyson Boyer

ACKNOWLEDGEMENTS

It is impossible to thank all those to whom I owe a debt of gratitude. No person has made a bigger sacrifice than Kathy, my wife, and our four children, Hilary, Trammell, Clara, and Melanie, who not only sacrificed time in the present, but who also sacrificed so that I could attend seminary.

Since graduating from seminary, I have served two congregations, First Presbyterian Church, Brownsville, Tennessee, and Advent Presbyterian Church, Cordova, Tennessee. Both congregations allowed me to be a student as well as a pastor, and have put up with the occasional deaf emotional ear of the preoccupied thinker. Both have been supportive of their pastor and forgiving of mistakes. For this, I thank them. Dave Schieber, my co-pastor, has the gift of encouragement (and patience), gifts he uses daily with me!

The manuscript was read by, among others, Rev. Warner Davis, and his wife, Ting Ting. Warner was a constant friend and encourager during the entire process. He is currently writing a book on his years growing up in the Congo. Marc Wiegand, an old friend from Texas, gave constant support and constructive advice, especially regarding the Introduction. Dr. Kendra Hotz, Peter Mascolo, Marianne McKee, Cassandra Moriarty, Dr. Teresa Waters, and her husband, Chris, Sara Robertson, and her husband, Fred, Mary Wilson, and her husband, Hon. Randy Wilson, and my good friend and long-time colleague, Dr. Cindy Schwartz and her husband, Jonathan, also gave valuable help and assistance. Thanks to everyone for your comments, criticisms, and encouragement.

There are many others who have given support, inspiration, love, and correction. I agree with Aristotle: a life without friendship is not a life worth living. Thanks to each and every one of you.

CONTENTS

PREFACE

A PERSONAL STORY

Many years ago, while an undergraduate philosophy major, I purchased a copy of the *Tao Te Ching*. As a lapsed Christian, the book meant little to me. Although I liked the exotic ring of the title, I did not take time to internalize the text. Almost thirty-five years later, as an orthodox Christian pastor of evangelical leanings, my old, largely unread copy of the *Tao Te Ching* fell at my feet.

At the time, I was grappling with a problem and looking in my closet library for a book I thought might be helpful. As a passing fancy, I opened the book and began to read. I was immediately drawn to a wise piece of advice, which guided me as I worked through the problem. This began a new love affair with *Tao Te Ching*.

During a quiet time each day, one of my disciplines is to choose a proverb as a guide to meditation. When I began reading the *Tao Te Ching*, the similarities between the teachings of Lao Tzu and the Wisdom literature of the Old Testament were immediately apparent. As I began studying the *Tao Te Ching*, I was forcibly struck by the many parallels between the teachings of the *Tao* and the feel and content of the teachings of Jesus, especially the wisdom of the Sermon on the Mount.

Soon, I began to paraphrase the wisdom of the *Tao Te Ching*. Armed with enthusiasm, but little experience in writing, I began work. I tried as best I could to find a way to make Eastern wisdom accessible to Christian laypeople, and especially to busy, responsible, laypeople. This book is the result of that process.

I have tried to adapt the basic principles of the Tao in expressly Christian terms. I have followed the original eighty-one chapter format, staying as close to the intention and feel of the *Tao Te Ching* as possible. The result is not the *Tao Te Ching*; it is a Christian adaptation of the book.

Early on, a pastor read a draft and suggested that my work was best directed toward Christian leaders. This pastor, who, of course, has leadership responsibilities in his congregation, saw the relevance of the *Tao Te Ching* for pastoral leadership. I reflected his comments in the work.

Later on, my wife, Kathy, read the manuscript. Her advice was the opposite of my friend. Many Christians do not think of themselves as leaders. She felt the book needed a wider audience because many people desire to grow spiritually and deepen the impact of their faith on their day-to-day Christian life. In her view, the book needed to be written for everyone. I rewrote the book with her comments in mind.

While on vacation, a friend reviewed the manuscript and asked me a question, "Chris. Could you please tell me what you are trying to say in three sentences?" I had a difficult time answering. I was so immersed in the details of the project that I lost sight of its core. My friend's question forced me to rethink what I was doing and spend time focusing the project.

The result of these comments is captured in the title, "Centered Living/Centered Leading". The book is about day to day living and, like the *Tao Te Ching*, it often touches on the specific demands of leadership.

The Goal: Better Balanced Christians and Leaders

The goal of the book is to help Christ-Followers, and especially Christian leaders, live wisely. Christians benefit from developing the capacity for deep wisdom, self-sacrificial love, prayer, meditation, simplicity of life, and peaceableness as they seek to serve other people. Pondering the way of living described by the *Tao Te Ching* and *Bible* can help immensely in this process.

Centered Living/Centered Leading: The Way of Light and Love will immediately appeal to those who need it least: those for whom meditation comes easy, for whom the importance of love in all of life seems obvious, and for those whose personalities and occupations make simplicity and moderation accomplishable without difficulty.

I hope such people enjoy this adaptation and profit from it, but it is not my intention to attract only those who are naturally attracted to prayer, meditation and simplicity. I hope to attract people like me: hyperactive, over-achievers who need to slow down. I also hope the book will attract another sort of person: the successful secular person who feels that their daily life and leadership fall short of being fully integrated with their spiritual life.

Before I went to seminary, I practiced law. For most of my career I practiced a kind of law requiring long hours, constant stress, and ceaseless activity. As I look back upon those years, one fact strikes me: *The worst mistakes I made were the result of fatigue combined with a failure to stop, seek the simplest path, and await revelation of a better way to solve a problem.*

What I lacked was what the *Tao Te Ching* suggests: the ability to meditate, seek the path of least disruption, and await a revelation from outside myself and outside the problem. I wrote this book partially as a kind of penance, with the hope that others may do better.

The *Tao Te Ching* contains a lot of advice applicable to leaders and to the process of leading. This advice is, however, directed not so much at what we *do* as it is directed toward who we *are* as leaders. It leads us to ask the question, "*Is who I am* and *what I do* consistent with what I profess to believe about the ultimate nature of reality?

In some ways, the *Tao Te Ching* and *Bible* are two great texts of "Servant Leadership." Trivial leaders manipulate people in the search for power and success. They are not real leaders. They are shrewd manipulators. They are not attempting to *serve* those they lead, but to *use* them for their own personal benefit.

Real, transforming leaders embody the ideals they proclaim. This should especially be true of leaders who are Christ-Followers. Christians are called to embody the personhood we proclaim to others, the personhood revealed in Jesus Christ. We are called to embody a wisdom that the world could not possibly know without God's self-disclosure in Christ (I Corinthians 2:6–8). When Christ-Followers embody the "Way of Jesus," then, and only then, can we lead others in a transforming way.

Going back to the day the *Tao Te Ching* fell off my bookshelf illustrates the point. At that moment, I was embroiled in a difficult conflict. My mind was on discerning a means to overcome those who, in my view, were undermining the health of an organization. Yet, I was too engaged in the conflict to see the limits wisdom placed on my actions.

The Biblical reminder of the power of love, and the Taoist warning concerning going too far in conflict, gave. me a new perspective. The *Tao Te Ching* reminded me to worry more about the kind of person I was becoming and less about the objective I was seeking.

The Spirituality and Morality of the Way

Basic Insights

Centered Living/Centered Leading: The Way of Light and Love, like the *Tao Te Ching*, addresses the spiritual and moral aspects of life. In particular, it concerns how human beings can adapt their behavior to a morality inherent in The Way Things Are, to the moral order of the universe. Human beings who do not align their goals, objectives, and plans to this spiritual and moral order sooner or later create chaos.

Where are we to look for spiritual and moral principles to guide our action? They are not to be found in the rules and practices of institutional decision-making. Leaders cannot find them by the simple calculus of "What is the rate of return on this investment?" or "How many votes will this bill cost?" Moral and spiritual decision-making requires that leaders move our thought to a higher level—to the level of meaning and value.

For Christians, good decision-making requires that we emulate the One who said that leadership within his kingdom was not about power, pride, or position, but about service (See Mark 10:35–45; Matthew 20:20–28; Luke 22:24–26). The Way of Jesus is the way of service in the spirit of self-giving love.

The dilemma for Christ-Followers is how to discern and apply the wisdom of Christ and the Christian tradition in an ever-changing and often challenging environment. Something like a "Tao of Christ" can help develop an attitude and approach that opens us to the Spirit of Jesus and the resources needed to solve day-to-day problems.

ANSWERING POTENTIAL OBJECTIONS

Some people may object to this adaptation of the *Tao Te Ching* for the reason that one ought to let each religious tradition stand on its own ground. In the Bibliography I list some of the many translations of the *Tao Te Ching* available in bookstores or over the Internet. I encourage anyone who enjoys this book to continue his or her study from the original text. Yet, there are those who will read this book who might never be exposed to the original text. For those people, I hope I am providing a service.

I also anticipate a complaint from another quarter. Some people may suggest that I am engaged in religious syncretism, bringing together Taoism and Christianity into a kind of religious "Mulligan Stew." In response, I can only say that my attempt has been to adapt the *Tao Te Ching* from the perspective of an orthodox Christian who works and thinks in the Reformed tradition. My goal was to explore the similarities between the two traditions while ultimately remaining loyal to my own.

This book *is* an attempt to enter into a kind of inter-religious dialogue with Taoism. The kind of discussion I have in mind involves appreciating another tradition while steadfastly maintaining the distinctive beliefs of one's own tradition.[1] When we have confidence in the truth of Christian faith, we are free to

---

1   See, John B. Cobb, Jr. *Beyond Dialogue: Toward a Mutual Transformation of Christianity and Buddhism* (Philadelphia, PA: Fortress Press, 1982): 17. The search for religious truth and wisdom is present in all religious traditions. Therefore, Christians, who worship the One who is "The Way, The Truth, and the Life," should applaud and welcome insights in other traditions that illuminate the nature and being of God revealed in Christ. It is in this spirit that I have tried to look at the wisdom of the East through a Christian lens.

accept and to value all truth. As the great Methodist missiologist E. Stanley Jones put it, "I was free, free to explore, to appropriate any good, any truth found elsewhere, for I belonged to the Truth, to Jesus Christ."[2] Christ-Followers should not fearfully reject other religions. All religions reflect the search for the One who is the Way, Truth, and Life. As such, whatever truth they embody is a part of the great Truth we proclaim.

THE WAY OF DEEP LIGHT AND DEEP LOVE

The Way of Deep Light

People often think of "faith" as holding something to be true on inadequate knowledge or in the face of contrary facts. Critics of Christianity sometimes describe faith as irrational, a flight from reason. For these people, "faith" means holding to a belief despite the absence of evidence, or worse, against clear evidence.

The false separation of faith and reason is foreign to the spirit of the writers of the Christian *Bible* and of the early Church. For early Christians, the wisdom Christ embodied was same divine wisdom revealed in nature (Romans 1:20). The revelation of Christ was a moment of deepened understanding of God and the universe God created. The early Church saw the Incarnation of Jesus Christ as a physical revelation of the invisible wisdom of God in the form of a human being (Colossians 1:15–17).

In the Judeo-Christian tradition, the fool (unwise) and the wicked (those who habitually violate the moral law) act against the grain of the Cosmos, against the rational order of Creation, and against the moral order God imbedded in human nature. The wise person faces this reality and lives according to reason and the moral

2   E. Stanley Jones, *A Song of Ascents* (Nashville, TN: Abingdon Press, 1968):92.

law. This moral order is summarized in the Great Commandment to love God and others. The practical implication of the Great Commandment is seen in the life of Jesus Christ.

Those who accept this ancient way of wisdom understand that scientific knowledge, faith, and moral insight are parts of a seamless web of created rationality binding the physical, moral, and intellectual universe together. Eugene Peterson captures this notion when he writes, *". . . God's law is not something alien, imposed on us from without, but woven into the very fabric of our creation. There is something deep within . . . that echoes God's yes and no, right and wrong"* (Romans 2:14 [Message]).

Frankly, it is important to reacquaint people with this older tradition, a tradition that sees moral inquiry and ethical decision-making as an attempt to bring human life to wholeness. This wholeness is achieved as the rational moral nature of the universe is reflected in the lives of concrete human beings who are attempting to live wisely and well. The wise life is not something we *create* by decision (as in existentialism and postmodernism). We *discover* the wise life by observation and meditation on reality in light of God's revelation in Christ.

In a world where many people have lost confidence in the existence of truth, it is important for Christ-Followers to humbly make known the Gospel as communicating real truth about the way the world is and its relation to its Creator. In a world where many people consider religion as something backward, it is important to keep in mind that Christians have always believed in the search for truth in whatever form, for God is the author of all truth. In a world where many people think of Christians as captured by superstition, it is important for Christians to proclaim Jesus Christ and him crucified, not against the facts, but as the way to make sense of the human condition and God's interaction with human beings. [3]

This has practical implications for Christ-Followers. Following Jesus is a discipline by which we consciously open our minds and hearts to the deep wisdom of God revealed in Christ. If, as Christians believe, Jesus embodies the wisdom of God, then true wisdom, wherever found, deepens our understanding of Christ. The *Tao Te Ching* is full of this kind of wisdom. It contains an understanding of life that can deepen our Christian understanding of the riches and depth of the wisdom of God and help us to live more authentically as Christians.

The Way of Deep Love

As the Apostles, New Testament writers, and early Christians meditated on the life, death, and resurrection of Jesus, they came to understand Jesus as God in human form—embodied Divine Love. One of the earliest names for Christians was "those who belong to the 'Way'" (Acts 9:2). Jesus showed his disciples both a way to fellowship with God and a way of life. The Beatitudes are a beautiful description of that Way. This Way of Jesus involves serving and leading others with a gentle, other-centered, sacrificial love.

There is a technical word for God's willingness to serve creation at its deepest point of need. The word is *kenosis*, which means "to empty." It comes from the words of Paul:

> Your attitude should be the same as that of Christ Jesus:
> Who, being in very nature God, did not consider equality
> with God something to be grasped, but made himself
> nothing, taking the very nature of a servant, being made

3   See, Lesslie Newbigin, *Truth To Tell: The Gospel as Public Truth* (Grand Rapids, MI & Geneva Switzerland: William B. Eerdmans and the World Council of Churches, 1991).

in human likeness. And being found in appearance as a man, he humbled himself and became obedient to death— even death on a cross! (Philippians 2:5-8[NIV]).

In the older translations, the phrase "made himself nothing" (*ekenosen*) is translated "emptied himself."This is the classic testimony to God's self-giving nature.

Christ reveals the limitless, vulnerable, self-giving love of God. In Christ, God serves the greatest need of human beings and creation by emptying himself of overt power in order to redeem them. The message of the Cross is that God is the One who gives himself without limit, without restriction, without any holding back for the sake of his broken creation and his sinful people.[4]

This is what Christians mean when we say, "God is love" (I John 4:8). The love of God patiently bears with us, even as we presume upon the mercy of God. The love of God endures our sin, our shortcomings, and our brokenness, as the Spirit works patiently and in love to redeem and restore. The Way of Christ begins in trusting this revelation, as Christians follow the example of the Christ in daily life.

THE WAY OF MEDITATION, SIMPLICITY, AND RESTRAINT
The Way of Meditation

How can Christians embody wisdom and compassionate action in our day-to-day lives? It is not easy. It will not happen unless we

---

4   See, W. H. Vanstone, *Love's Endeavor, Love's Expense: the Response of Being to the Love of God* (London, UK: Darton, Longman and Todd, 1977). See also, John Polkinghorne, ed, *The Work of Love: Creation as Kenosis* (Grand Rapids, MI: Eerdmans 2001) for a deep analysis of how creation reflects the One who is love and became love incarnate to redeem and restore his handiwork.

develop appropriate spiritual habits, especially the habits of daily prayer and meditation, simplicity of life, and self-restraint.

We live in a culture in which most people live frenetic, complex, overly active lives. We are prone to big, dramatic solutions to complex problems, solutions which even the most sophisticated thinkers, do not fully understand. The result is growing social, religious, political, and cultural chaos. We need to learn to appreciate a better, wiser, older way.

Servant leaders need a deep awareness of available options and the foresight to understand where a chosen course of action will lead.[5] This kind of awareness is difficult to achieve unless one develops a habit of thoughtful meditation.[6] This is, unfortunately, a habit our culture has largely lost.

As Christianity grew and became embedded in Roman society, it was not long before the prayer life of the church began to suffer. In response, ancient believers developed a Christian form of meditation and contemplation. The church developed a way of seeking the Deep Light by withdrawing from the world of the senses and meditating on Scripture. The goal was to seek a deep connection with the One who is both Deep Love and Deep Light, in order to live a transformed life.

For Christ-Followers, meditation opens the human psyche to the Holy Spirit. It is a way of prayerfully inviting God into the depth of our human problems and allowing Christ to speak to us at the deepest level of our being.

---

5   Robert K. Greenleaf, *Servant Leadership: A Journey into the Nature of Legitimate Power and Greatness* (Mahwah, NY: Paulist Press, 1991):21-28.

6   The habit of meditation is a tool for openness to communication with Christ, a habit which arises from Christian prayer.

The Way of Simplicity

Author Richard Foster begins his book, *Freedom of Simplicity*, by observing that "the lust for affluence in contemporary society has become psychotic."[7] As hard as it is to accept his conclusion, the desire for an increasing variety of possessions, and the greed for additional money that goes along with the desire for more possessions, is a major problem for contemporary people. At some point, the acquisition, maintenance, and replacement of things becomes a barrier to authentic spiritual and emotional wholeness. It prevents true, compassionate living and the kind of leadership that flows from emotional and spiritual well-being.

Only those who embrace simplicity can minister to the deepest need of our culture, which is to learn contentment with enough. Simplicity is not denying oneself necessary things; it is having the wisdom to have, maintain, and replace necessary and important things, while rejecting the message contained in so much advertising that things themselves provide contentment, joy, and peace. They do not.

The Way of Restraint

Finally, our society breeds a kind of complex hyperactivity that can result in Christians mistaking *activity* for *progress*. The *Tao Te Ching* often speaks of the virtue of *Wu Wei*, or "no action". Over and over again, the *Tao Te Ching* advises people to exercise restraint, await a revelation of wisdom in unfolding circumstances, and act in a way that involves the least disturbance.

The path of wisdom urges us to be still, to be patient, to listen, to be open, not to rush, to be suspicious of the urge to rapidly overcome resistance. In essence, the way of wisdom leads us to remain open to the mystery of the Holy Spirit. The Way suggests

7   Richard J. Foster *Freedom of Simplicity* (San Francisco, CA: Harper & Row, 1981): 3.

a radical caution, as opposed to arrogant certainty in which action overruns difficulties. The Way avoids a hubris which disregards the quiet voice of the Holy Spirit.

The humble approach of the *Tao Te Ching* and Biblical faith is completely at odds with our preference for "Big Plans" to solve "Big Problems" quickly. All over the world, leaders over-promise followers. The wise leader is satisfied to seek the good in current circumstances, to solve problems with the least disruption, and to restrain his or her messianic impulse to play the part of the "Great Leader."

CONCLUSION

Like most avid readers, I tend to read books quickly. *Centered Living/Centered Leading* should not be read in this way. Wisdom literature must be read slowly, meditated upon, and internalized. Readers who read only a chapter or so each day and digest its message before moving onto the next chapter will receive the greatest blessing from the book.

In order to make internalization easier, Bible verses, a short commentary covering at least one point of the text, and questions are included. For readers who desire to know more about the *Tao Te Ching* there is an introduction included before the adaptation. In any case, I wish every reader well. I hope this little book will be as much fun to read as it was for the author to prepare.

One last word: many Christians do not think of themselves as "leaders". My wife, who first raised this problem, is a mother of four and teacher. Other mothers, one with six children, also read drafts of this book. Three professors, a judge, two pastors and a retired business person reviewed drafts of the book. All of these people are, in fact, leaders in their families, congregations, workplaces, and communities. We are all leaders, and we all need the wisdom of Christ as we conduct our day to day lives.

Blessings to all who undertake the journey this book encourages.

Chris Scruggs
All Saints Day, 2009

THE TAO, CHRISTIAN LIFE AND LEADERSHIP

LAO TZU AND THE *TAO TE CHING*

The wisdom of the Tao is older than the *Tao Te Ching*. The writer of the *Tao Te Ching* did not pretend to form a new religion. Instead, he set out fundamental principles of a way of life that already existed. So, he writes, "Wield the Tao of the ancients to manage the existence of today."[8] The Tao is as old as human interaction with the ultimate ground of life and virtue. It did not begin with the *Tao Te Ching*.

No one really knows when the given author, Lao Tzu, lived, if he lived, or if he was the writer of the *Tao Te Ching*. It is possible that "Lao Tzu" is simply a name given to wisdom collected by ancient Chinese sages; something like what scholars believe happened when Proverbs was collected and its wisdom ascribed to Solomon. This notion is given some credence by the name itself, which translates, "Old Master" or "Old Sage".

According to legend, Lao Tzu was a librarian in the court of the Zhou dynasty. He may have lived during what is known as "the Warring States Period". This was a time of social decay and violence.

Concerned about the condition of society, Lao Tzu determined to leave his position and withdraw from active life. Legend has it that, as he was leaving his home, a guard commander, recognized him, stopped him at a border, and asked him to write down his wisdom. He did so in eighty-one short chapters. Once the task was

---

8   Lao Tzu, *Tao Te Ching: Annotated and Explained* tr. Derek Lin Chapter 14 (Woodstock, VT: Skylight Press, 2006): 29.

completed, Lao Tzu continued his journey and disappeared from history.

The book "Lao Tzu" left behind is a classic text of human wisdom and the foundational book of Taoism. The *Tao Te Ching* has had an important influence on Chinese culture. Its concepts impacted the development of Confucianism, as well as the general cultural heritage of modern China. Despite the upheavals of the Twentieth Century, the *Tao Te Ching* is a force in Chinese thought and has impacted other cultures as well. For example, because of the interest of many film and media persons in Taoism and Eastern religions, Western popular culture is affected by Taoist ideas.

The word *Tao* (pronounced "Dao") means "Way" or "Path" and is a fundamental concept of Chinese philosophy. The underlying notion is that of "method," "truth," "principle," or even "reality".[9] C. S. Lewis describes the role of the *Tao* in Chinese thought: "It is the reality beyond all predicates, the abyss that was before the Creator Himself. It is Nature, the Way, and the Road. It is the Way in which the universe goes on, the way in which things everlasting emerge, stilly and tranquilly, into space and time. It is also the Way which every human being should tread in imitation of that cosmic and super-cosmic progression, conforming all activities to that great exemplar."[10] It is what in Christian terms we might call the "Natural Law" or the "Ways of God."

The *Tao Te Ching* does not tell us about God, Jesus, or the Holy Spirit. The *Tao Te Ching* tells us about the human condition and about how to live wisely on the path to greater wholeness. Inherent in its

---

9   Wing-Tsit Chan, *The Way of Lao Tzu (Tao Te Ching)* tr. Wing Tsit Chan. (New York, Mcmillan, 1963): 6.

10   C. S. Lewis, *The Abolition of Man* (New York, Collier Books, a division of Macmillan, 1955): 28.

teachings is the notion that life is full of problems and wisdom comes from finding a proper response to those problems.

The *Tao Te Ching* primarily presents to us an attitude toward life. It is about stillness and waiting, taking the path of least resistance, and choosing the course of least disruption to society and others. It describes a way of being in the world and a method for dealing with the "problems of life." The *Tao Te Ching*, then, is a "manual" that provides a method by which we can successfully address ourselves to the human condition and the challenges we human beings face.

Tao Te Ching and Christian Thought Distinguished

There are many instances where the wisdom of *Tao Te Ching* and the *Bible* agree. Yet, there are important differences between the fundamental presuppositions of Christianity and Taoism. As one reads the *Tao Te Ching*, it is important to keep in mind the differences between the two systems of belief.

An Imminent verses Transcendent Wisdom

The fundamental distinction between Taoism and the Judea-Christian tradition concerns the nature of Ultimate Reality. In Taoism, the mystical experience involves coming to a deeper understanding of wisdom imbedded in the world. The Tao is the "matrix," or ground, from which all things emerge. It is simply the Way Things Are.

Christians self-consciously believe in what Francis Schaeffer calls the "Infinite Personal God."[11] The infinite God is the Creator of the Heavens and the Earth, yet transcends creation. While Christians do not deny the immanent nature of wisdom—its grounding in

---

11   Francis Schaeffer, "The God who is There" in *The Complete Works of Francis Schaeffer: A Christian World View* Vol. I 2nd ed. (Wheaton, Ill: Crossway Books, 1982).

the way the world is—Christians believe that prudent living is not possible without a wisdom grounded in the transcendent reality of God.

For those who worship a transcendent God, the quest for wisdom involves respectful contemplation of the Creator God as well as God's creation (Proverbs 9:10). Reflection on created reality is not enough to discern the boundaries of the wise life, since created reality points toward a Divine Reality. This Divine Reality is the ground of created reality. Humans are limited in what they can know in any field of endeavor. Therefore, final, complete explanation can be found only in the transcendent God who is the Creator and Sustainer of all things.[12]

An Impersonal versus a Personal Ultimate Reality

Christians also believe that God is ultimately *personal*. The Doctrine of the Trinity conceives of God as Father, Son, and Holy Spirit, a relational unity of being. Ultimate reality is essentially *relational* and *personal*. Therefore, it can only be known relationally and personally.

Christians believe that "God is love" (1 John 4:8). This Divine Love became incarnate in the person of Jesus of Nazareth and "dwelt among us full of grace and truth" (John 1:14 [NIV]). For Christ-Followers, in Jesus Christ, the Light (wisdom) of God and the Love (self-sacrificing relationality) of God were joined together in an indissoluble unity. The Eternal Word (Logos), the ground of the rationality of the created universe, is, at its core, Divine

---

12   This difference in fundamental orientation makes a good deal of difference in the nature of wisdom. Human reflection on creation has its ground in the One God, the "Maker of Heaven and Earth," who created the rational order of our universe yet transcends it. For Christ-Followers, wise living ultimately has a transcendent ground in a Triune, Relational God of Light (Truth), and Love (Self-giving Relationality).

Love. Thus, among other things, the incarnation of the Word binds together the *rational* world of truth and the *relational* world of love.

For Christ-Followers, the Triune God exists in love and displays love toward all creation. Wisdom, when it is found, leads to a life of compassionate, loving service to others. As a friend of mine put it, the revelation of Christ discloses that "Love is the most rational act of all."[13]

An Unknowable or Knowable Ultimate Reality

In Taoism, the nature of the Tao is mysterious and unknowable. Thus, "The Tao that can be told is not the eternal Tao" and "The thing that is called the Tao is eluding and vague".[14] Whatever the nature of ultimate reality, it cannot be known by finite human beings.

For Christians, the ultimate reality of the universe is a Personal God who became incarnate in Christ Jesus. Thus, Ultimate Reality is not a complete mystery in the sense that human beings cannot know *any* real truth about it. Indeed, because of Christ, we can know the most important truth concerning its nature—that "God is love" (I John 4:8).

This makes a difference in the way Christians and Taoists look at the nature of ultimate reality. In the Cross, Christian believers see revealed the ultimate truth of the Universe—that God is sacrificial love. This Divine Love is "cruciform love" in which God personally bears the sin and suffering of the world in a great act of

---

13   Rev. Dr. Warner Davis, pastor of the Collierville Presbyterian Church in Collierville, Tennessee in a private conversation, May 24, 2007. Warner read several drafts of this document.

14   Wing-Tsit Chan, *The Way of Lao Tzu (Tao-te Ching)* tr. Wing-Tsit Chan (New York: Macmillian, 1963): Chapters I & 21.

redemption.[15] The Cross reveals the hidden, paradoxical wisdom of God, the wisdom of the One who said, "If anyone would come after me, let him deny himself and take up his cross and follow me" (Matthew 16:24 [ESV]).

Christians believe sacrificial love is part of the deepest order of the universe. For early Christians, the revelation embodied in Jesus was not a flight into the irrational or the subjective world of metaphor. Instead, Christ provided a revelatory insight into the deepest rationality of the world.

This is why an early Christian could say, "He is the image of the invisible God, the firstborn of all creation; for in him all things in heaven and on earth were created, things visible and invisible, whether thrones or dominions or rulers or powers—all things have been created through him and for him. He himself is before all things, and in him all things hold together." (Colossians 1:15–17 [NRSV]).[16]

---

15 For those who believe in a transcendent God, it is not enough to conform thinking and action to a reason immanent in creation or human nature. Even the deepest meditation on the created order can take us only so far. Only through the mystery of the Cross can reality be accurately perceived. Moreover, only by following in the way of the Cross can we adjust our behavior to this reality.

16 This way of thinking reached its peak in the Gospel of John, where the Apostle writes, "In the beginning was the Word, and the Word was with God, and the Word was God. He was in the beginning with God. All things were made through Him, and without Him nothing was made that was made. In Him was life, and the life was the light of men. And the light shines in the darkness, and the darkness did not comprehend it" (John 1:1–5 [NKJV]). In this introduction to his Gospel, John understands that, in Jesus of Nazareth, "the true Light, which enlightens everyone, was coming into the world" (John 1:9 [NRSV]). Thus, John equates the incarnate Christ with the Eternal Logos of Greek thought..

COMMON TEACHINGS

Despite fundamental differences between Taoism and Christianity, even a casual reader is struck by many areas of agreement. Here are just a few areas where a sympathetic reader sees commonality between the teachings of the *Tao Te Ching* and Christianity:

Compassionate Love

The section of the *Tao Te Ching* that first caught my eye read: "When Heaven is to save a person, Heaven will protect him through deep love."[17] The thought is almost identical to the most quoted verse in Scripture, John 3:16, "For God so loved the world that he gave his one and only Son, that whoever believes in him shall not perish but have eternal life."

In Christian thinking the greatest virtue is self-giving, sacrificial, agape love for others (I Corinthians 13). While the Taoist notion of "deep love" and the Christian notion of God's self-giving love are not identical, both point to the need for compassionate self-sacrifice in human relationships. Both the Tao and Christianity recognize that deep love involves sacrificial caring.

Meditation and Contemplation

Taoism and Christianity agree that meditation and contemplation are important to wise living. One cannot follow the Tao by mere activity, even by mental, cognitive activity. Meditation is required. Thus, in the *Tao Te Ching*, it is taught:

> If you can empty your mind of all thoughts
> your heart will embrace the tranquility of peace.

---

17   Win-Tsit Chan, *Tao Te Ching*, chapter 67, p. 219.

> Watch the workings of all of creation,
> but contemplate their return to the source.[18]

The Tao (Way) is known as we enter a state of tranquility and open ourselves to reality.

While Christians believe there is an active way to achieve wisdom through Bible study and verbal prayer, there is also tradition that emphasizes meditation and contemplation.[19] So the Psalmist speaks of meditating on the *Torah* (law) day and night (Psalm 1:2).

Meditation is a process of prayerfully reflecting and pondering God's revelation. It has an active component as we meditate upon the revelation of Christ, the Eternal Word of God, and upon the word of Holy Scripture. On the other hand, meditation involves a passive "resting in God" or "lovingly gazing upon God," a knowing beyond knowing.[20]

Christ-Followers understand the value of quiet meditation in seeking an appropriate response to problems and opportunities. In meditation, we bring together the revelation of Christ with the objective content of Holy Scripture and the concrete realities of a particular situation. In contemplation, we open ourselves to the silent instruction of the Holy Spirit who instructs the heart concerning the best response to the problems of life.

---

18   Lao Tzu, *Tao Te Ching - A Translation For the Public Domain.* Chapter 14. J. H. McDonald www.Wrighthouse.com/religions/taoism (1996).

19   Psalms makes frequent mention of the need for meditation and contemplation upon the Torah and upon the One who gave Israel the Torah. Psalm 131 teaches the need for silence and for a kind of openness to God when it says, "My heart is not proud, O LORD, my eyes are not haughty; I do not concern myself with great matters or things too wonderful for me. But I have stilled and quieted my soul; like a weaned child with its mother, like a weaned child is my soul within me" (Psalm (131:1–2 [NIV]).

20   Thelma Hall, *Too Deep for Words: Rediscovering Lectio Divina* (Mahwah, NJ: Paulist Press, 1988): 9.

Humility

Taoism and Christianity agree that humility is important to the wise life. Lowliness, humility, and contentment with the human condition are fundamental to the Taoist ethic:

> The best of people is like Water
> Water gives life to all things
> And does not compete with them.
> It flows to places people reject
> And so is like the Tao.[21]

In Taoism, the prudent person recognizes his or her solidarity with the earth and the humblest human beings. Humility is necessary for those who would guide people wisely: "If the sage would guide the people, he must serve with humility."[22] It is by accepting our human limitations that we become wise.

Christianity also recognizes the virtue of humility. In Proverbs, we read, "When pride comes, then comes disgrace; but wisdom is with the humble" (Proverbs 11:2 [NRSV]). In the Sermon on the Mount, Jesus proclaims, "Blessed are the meek, for they will inherit the earth" (Matthew 5:5 [NRSV]). In First Peter, the author teaches, "You should all clothe yourselves with humility toward one another, because God sets his face against the arrogant but shows favor toward the humble" (1 Peter 4:5b [REV]).

Humility involves eliminating pride and prejudice. This attitude allows us to see situations and others sympathetically. When we are humble, we recognize that whatever our station in life, whatever our achievements, we are still human, still fragile, still finite. Thus

---

21   Martin Aronson, ed. *Jesus and Lao Tzu: The Parallel Sayings* (Berkeley, CA: Seastone Press, 2000): 55.

22   *Id*, at 59. Over and over again in the *Tao Te Ching* the virtue of humility and its importance in gaining wisdom is emphasized.

humbled, we are open to the secret wisdom God imparts to the humble—and to the humble alone.

Patience and Peaceableness

Christianity and Taoism share an aversion toward violence, a respect for gentleness, and a desire to secure peace. Lao Tzu says, "Violent and fierce people do not die a natural death.' I shall make this the father of my teaching."[23] Although the *Tao Te Ching* recognizes the reality of war, it discourages armed conflict.

Thus, "When Tao prevails in the world, galloping horses are turned back to fertilize (fields with their dung). When the Tao does not prevail in the world, war horses thrive in the suburbs."[24] Conflict and violence may be inevitable parts of the human condition, but they are to be avoided whenever possible.

Gentleness, contentment, and peaceableness lead to a preference for patience over ceaseless seeking and activity. Therefore the *Tao Te Ching* teaches: "The Tao abides in non-action, yet nothing is left undone."[25] This is a warning that ceaseless activity is destructive of the finest human potentialities, and selfish desire causes conflict.

Tenderness, contentment and peaceableness are also crucial to Christian life. Jesus says, "Blessed are the peacemakers, for they will be called the children of God" (Matthew 5:9 [NRSV]). [26] Those who are always striving to have more, to control more,

---

23   Win-Tsit Chan, *The Way of Lao Tzu (Tao Te Ching)* tr. Win Tsit Chan *(New York, NY: McMillian, 1963)*, chapter 42, p. 176.

24   Id, chapter 46, 181.

25   Lao Tzu, *Tao Te Ching* Chapter 37. tr. Gia Fu-Feng & Jane English. int. Jacob Needleman (New York, NY: Vintage Books, 1989):39.

26   James also views greed as underlying causes of conflict and war: "What causes fights and quarrels among you? Don't they come from your desires that battle within you?" (James 4:11 [NIV]).

and to dominate others have embraced a foolish, and ultimately destructive, style of living.

Simplicity

Both Taoism and Christianity see simplicity as central to the wise life. The wise person lives simply, and by embracing simplicity, achieves contentment. Just after talking about the scourge of war, Lao Tzu says:

> There is no calamity greater than lavish desires.
> There is no guilt greater than discontentment.
> There is no greater disaster than greed.[27]

Similarly, the Old and New Testaments warn against seeking excessive possessions. In the New Testament, Jesus warns against worrying about possessions:

And why do you worry about clothes? See how the lilies of the field grow. They do not labor or spin. Yet I tell you that not even Solomon in all his splendor was dressed like one of these. If that is how God clothes the grass of the field, which is here today and tomorrow is thrown into the fire, will he not much more clothe you, O you of little faith? So do not worry, saying, 'What shall we eat?' or 'What shall we drink?' or 'What shall we wear?' For the pagans run after all these things, and your heavenly Father knows that you need them. But seek first his kingdom and his righteousness, and all these things will be given to you as well (Matthew 6:28–33 [NIV]).

We live in a time in which the message that possessions and material goods cannot, by themselves, create happiness or the "good

---

27   Win-Tsit Chan, *Tao Te Ching*, chapter 46, p. 181.

life," needs to be heard. We live in an age when people restlessly seek happiness and contentment in ever more complicated lives. The result is personal and social fragmentation. In the midst of the complexities of our culture, people need to ponder the importance of simplicity.

IMPLICATIONS FOR LEADERSHIP

The Leader as Servant

The *Tao Te Ching* and Biblical faith point to the same ethos for leaders. Human pride cannot create a heaven on earth. In fact, experience causes the prudent person to fear that pride will lead to suffering and oppression. The best kind of leadership involves service to others.

Both Christianity and Taoism are suspicious of the "Great Man" theory of history, and of our human capacity to create a heaven on earth. Programs, such as the "Great Society" or the "Great Leap Forward" often result in unforeseen consequences. Wise leaders, therefore, conform to a Way that transcends our human programs for human improvement. They avoid narcissistic pride.

Both the *Bible* and the *Tao Te Ching* urge leaders to serve those they lead. Americans are inevitably affected by our Western, democratic culture, and modern thought is deeply affected by the Nietzschean notion of the "Will to Power".[28] Too often, contemporary people

---

28 Nietchzsche's notion of the "Will to Power" and its relationship to modern notions of leadership is complex and easily over-simplified. Nietchzsche developed his notion of the Will to Power as both as an outgrowth of the impulsive and adventurous impulse of life and as a theory of aggressive self-assertive quest for power. See, George A. Morgan, *What Nietzsche Means* (New York, NY: Harper Torchbooks, 1965) for a complete discussion of this matter. Unfortunately, some leaders have consciously or unconsciously followed his philosophical and psychological insights to justify unrestrained self-assertion in leadership, which the *Bible* and the *Tao Te Ching* condemn.

fall into the comfortable notion that the correct response to problems is a matter of mere choice— either in the results of a public election or in the person of a popularly elected leader. This too often translates into the mistaken notion that the right course of action is whatever elites can persuade a majority of the population to support.

In opposition to self-centered, self-assertive leadership, the *Tao Te Ching* and the *Bible* encourage servant leadership. The *Tao Te Ching* teaches: "Giving birth, nourishing life, shaping things without possessing them, serving without expectation of reward, leading without dominating: These are the profound virtue of nature and of nature's best beings."[29] Jesus teaches, "If anyone wants to be first, he must be the very last and the servant of all" (Mark 9:35). The notion of servant leadership, popular even among secular leadership theorists, developed from these teachings of Jesus. This is a perspective our world desperately needs.

Leaders as Students of Inherited Wisdom

For Taoism and Christianity the right course of action in a particular situation is *found*, not merely *chosen* among alternatives. The solution to social, political, and economic problems is not *created* by human choice but *discovered* through a process of thought and investigation into the challenges faced and the possible alternatives. Leaders, therefore, must be students of nature and of human nature.

When decisions are required, meditation is required, or a foolish course of action will be chosen. Where choices must be made that affect the public interest, the spirit of humble service must be present, or the best interests of people will not be served. Where the potential for conflict is present, it must be avoided if

---

29   Lao Tzu, *The Tao Te Ching of Lao Tzu* tr. Brian Brown Walker (New York, NY: St. Martin's Press, 1995) Chapter 51.

possible. If it is not possible, the path of least violence should be chosen.

The Way of the Tao and the Christian Way both imply respect for people, for tradition, for institutions that already exist, and for solutions that are already implicitly in place. The Way of the Tao and the Way of Christ are not sympathetic to the Way of the Revolutionary, so popular in the modern world. The best leader is not the revolutionary who changes everything by the force of charisma but the leader who changes things so subtly that the people believe they accomplished the change on their own.[30]

Where do wise leaders look for underlying principles to guide their action? If the moral and scientific universes reflect an underlying rationality, then virtue is not found by simply living according to a particular culture's social customs, as important as customs are. Virtue involves embodying the rational, moral nature of the universe in a human life. If there is a deep underlying moral and spiritual order, then the wise leader must adapt his or her actions to the "warp and woof" of that order.

In the Hindu and Buddhist tradition, this ultimate moral reality is the "Dharma." In Chinese culture, the ultimate reality to which human beings must adjust their behavior is the "Tao." In Judeo-Christian thinking, this created moral nature of the universe is called "Natural Law"—the moral nature or character the Creator implanted into creation. Virtue is "Written upon the Heart" of the wise and well-formed person as his or her behavior embodies that moral order.[31] It is this Tao, this Natural Law, to which leaders must ultimately turn for guidance.

---

30 Thus, the Tao Te Ching teaches, "Therefore, guide others by quietly relying on Tao. When the work is done, the people can say, 'We did it ourselves.'" *Id*, at 17.
31 See J. Budziszewski, *Written on the Heart: The Case for Natural Law* (Downer's Grove, IL: InterVarsity Press, 1997):61. Modern people, under the influence of the Enlightenment

Leaders lead best when they embody the moral order in their lives and conform their actions to the principles, the moral and spiritual order, implanted in each and every human being, rich and poor, strong or weak, powerful or powerless. Primary among those principles are the demands of human reason and what the New Testament calls the "Law of Love" (See Mark 12:28–31; Matthew 22:34–40).

CONCLUSION

A Christian interaction with the *Tao Te Ching* is profitable both for Christians and for those impacted by the Taoist tradition. Both traditions point us to the importance of developing a form of life in harmony with the ultimate nature of reality and the way the world in fact operates. Both urge what Sir John Templeton called, "The Humble Approach," an approach to reality characterized by humility and a willingness to learn.[32] Where such an approach is taken, the dangers of hubris and pride are minimized, and the proper posture to achieve wisdom can be achieved.

Centered Living/Centered Leading can help ordinary Christians and Christian leaders deepen and strengthen their faith and walk as we assimilate the wisdom and virtues of the *Tao Te Ching*. The teachings of the *Tao Te Ching* are not a replacement for Scripture, which remains for Christians the final authority for faith and morals. But, pondering the *Tao Te Ching*, as I have done in this book, can flesh out for many people deeper implications of Christian faith for our lives today.

---

and its hostility to tradition and non-scientific ways of knowing, have largely lost the notion that morality is more than social custom or a "lifestyle" decision. Too often, modern people think moral and lifestyle choices are ultimately subjective.

32   See, John M. Templeton, *The Humble Approach: Scientists Discover God* (New York, NY Seabury Press, 1981).

Centered Living/Centered Leading

The Way of Light and Love

The Tao Te Ching adapted for Christ-Followers

"Wisdom has built her house,
She has hewn out her seven pillars;
She has slaughtered her meat,
She has mixed her wine,
She has also furnished her table.
She has sent out her maidens,
She cries out from the highest places of the city,
"Whoever *is* simple, let him turn in here!"
As for him who lacks understanding, she says to him,
"Come, eat of my bread
And drink of the wine I have mixed."
Proverbs 9:1-5

"It means," said Aslan," that though the Witch knew the Deep
Magic, there is magic deeper still which she did not know. Her
knowledge goes back only to the dawn of Time. But, if she could
have looked a little further back, into the stillness and darkness
before Time dawned, she would have read there a different
incantation."

C. S. Lewis, *The Lion, the Witch and the Wardrobe*

Chapter I

The Heavens and the Earth,
    visible things and invisible things,
        are the creation of the One Who Is.

The Word binds together Heaven and Earth.
The Uncreated Light of the Word
    was before all things, created all things.
The Word shines in all darkness:
    understanding begins here.
The Way of Jesus is the Eternal Way,
    the Way of the Eternal Word.

The Spirit is the Spirit of the Word.
The Creator Spirit was before all things
    with the Word and the One Who Is,
        bringing light to all things.

A heart bent by false desire
    cannot see the Word clearly.
A heart freed from wrongful desire
    sees the hidden mystery of the Word.

IN THE BEGINNING WAS THE WORD, AND THE WORD WAS WITH
GOD, AND THE WORD WAS GOD.
(John 1:1 [NRSV])

TO FIND THE WAY, BE FREE OF FALSE DESIRE

The original *Tao Te Ching* teaches that "the Tao that can be described is not the Eternal Tao." For the Taoist, the Ultimate is inherently unknowable. Although Christians agree that God is beyond complete human understanding, Christ-Followers believe the true Way *can* be seen and understood—in the revelation of Christ. This is why Jesus says, "I am the way, the truth and the life" (John 14:6). In Christ, Deep Light and Deep Love are joined in a single revelation. This revelation enables the human heart to respond to the mystery of God.

Both followers of the Tao and Christ-Followers believe that persons whose hearts are twisted by false desire cannot understand the Way to wholeness and wise living. An honorable life and a pure heart (moral virtue) are necessary for the intellect to comprehend and the heart to embrace the deeply True, Good and Beautiful. There is more to religious knowing than mere understanding. There is more to the good life than analytical reasoning can uncover. Only those who by faith commit to a life of wise loving service to others can actually achieve it.

Have you ever been driven by desire and made a mistake of judgment that harmed you or someone else? What happened? How would things have been different if you had been a different kind of person?

Chapter 2

The Word creates in Uncreated Love.
The Word creates by Uncreated Light.
All things reflect the One Who Is and Will Be:
    the beginning and the end,
        hard times and easy times,
            success and failure.

People with a vision of Truth recognize Falsehood.
People with a vision of Beauty recognize Ugliness.
People with a vision of the Good recognize Evil.

What must be comes—wise leaders do not resist.
Things that must depart leave—wise shepherds let them go.

The wise person acts without excessive struggle.
The wise person teaches without excessive talking.
The wise person possesses without grasping,
    acting toward passing things
        with modest hopes.

When the work of the wise leader is done,
    he or she takes no credit.
This is the Way of the Good Shepherd.

THEREFORE, I URGE YOU, BROTHERS AND SISTERS, IN VIEW OF
GOD'S MERCY, TO OFFER YOUR BODIES AS LIVING SACRIFICES, HOLY
AND PLEASING TO GOD THIS IS YOUR SPIRITUAL ACT OF WORSHIP.
DO NOT CONFORM ANY LONGER TO THE PATTERN OF THIS WORLD,
BUT BE TRANSFORMED BY THE RENEWING OF YOUR MIND. THEN
YOU WILL BE ABLE TO TEST AND APPROVE WHAT GOD'S WILL IS—
HIS GOOD, PLEASING AND PERFECT WILL.

(Romans 12: 1–2 [TNIV])

Be Transformed and Walk in the Way

Both Christianity and Taoism agree that fundamental values are
not arbitrary. They are not merely a matter of human or cultural
innovation. They are part of the order of things. For the Taoist,
Truth, Beauty, and Goodness reflect the Tao. By living in conformity
with the Tao, the Taoist achieves a balanced, truthful, and beautiful
life.

For Christ-Followers, Truth, Beauty and Goodness reflect the
character of God. Human beings, created in the image of God,
can reflect in their thinking and acting these divine attributes. In
fact, only by allowing God to transform our ways of thinking
and acting, can we become wise. A person who lives in the Way
of Christ learns to accept what comes, acting prudently in the
concrete circumstances of the moment. Those who have the gift
and responsibility of leadership especially need this virtue.

*Standards of beauty, moral behavior, and truth vary among cultures. What do
you think is the common source for these standards? How do you think you could
better embody a love of beauty, goodness and truth?*

CHAPTER 3

If leaders value only talent and natural ability,
    those they shepherd become overly competitive.
If leaders value material wealth above virtue,
    those they shepherd become greedy.

Do not pridefully show treasures to onlookers—
    those who see them will become envious
        and seek to acquire what is yours.
This creates unhealthy competition.

Wise leaders remember the Word and its Deep Light,
    removing unhealthy distractions
        and providing for the necessities of life.
In this way, wise shepherds
    allow their community to become strong in virtue.

Wise leaders prefer simplicity
    and are free from wrongful desires,
        avoiding the pitfalls of mere shrewdness,
            cunning, or violent action.

Those who rely on the Word
    wait patiently,
        taking only necessary actions.

IF YOU ARE WISE AND UNDERSTAND GOD'S WAYS, PROVE IT BY
LIVING AN HONORABLE LIFE, DOING GOOD WORKS WITH THE
HUMILITY THAT COMES FROM WISDOM.
(James 3:11-12 [NLT])

Be Wise and Humble

The greatest Old Testament leader, Moses, was "the most humble of men" (Numbers 12:3). Proverbs teaches, "When pride comes, then comes disgrace; but, with humility comes wisdom" (Proverbs 11:2). Jesus said, "Come to me, all you who are weary and burdened, and I will give you rest. Take my yoke upon you and learn from me, for I am gentle and humble in heart, and you will find rest for your souls. For, my yoke is easy and my burden is light" (Matthew 11:28-30). Jesus embodied true humility.

Becoming humble is the first step in becoming wise. When we become humble, we become teachable. We do not overreach. We do not show off or draw attention to ourselves. We are relieved of the great burden of our own pride and ambition. When we take on the "yoke" of the Man of Sorrows, we are relieved of the greatest burden we carry: our own self-centered pride.

The Way teaches that the wise person avoids unhealthy ambition.
What would this entail in your life? What would it mean for you
to live more humbly and simply?

Chapter 4

The One Who Is and Will Be
    hides in unfathomable darkness,
        but is always present in Deep Light.

Eternally begotten by Uncreated Light in Eternal Love,
    the Word is the eternal source and ground
        of all things and all life.

The Spirit unifies all creation,
    holding together creation by Deep Light,
        sustaining creation in Deep Love,
            illuminating hidden things.

The One Who Is, the Word, and the Spirit
    have no beginning and no end.
No one understands their beginning,
    for they always were.
No one understands their end,
    for they will always be.

This is the mystery of the Triune One.

WHERE CAN I GO FROM YOUR SPIRIT? OR WHERE CAN I FLEE FROM YOUR PRESENCE? ... IF I SAY, "SURELY THE DARKNESS SHALL COVER ME, AND THE LIGHT AROUND ME BECOME NIGHT," EVEN THE DARKNESS IS NOT DARK TO YOU; THE NIGHT IS AS BRIGHT AS THE DAY, FOR DARKNESS IS AS LIGHT TO YOU.

(Psalm 139:7, 11–12 [NRSV])

Ponder the Mysterious Source of All Things

For the Taoist, the Tao is the principle of creation. For the Christian, the Word of God, which became flesh in Jesus, is the deep, mysterious, rational source of all things. This Word is not something before God or created by God, but the Uncreated Light and Love of God upon which the created order is grounded.

The Word is reflected in the natural and moral order of the world, but it transcends the natural and moral order as a spiritual reality. "For by him all things were created: things in heaven and on earth, visible and invisible, whether thrones or powers or rulers or authorities; all things were created by him and for him. He is before all things, and in him all things hold together" (Colossians 1:16–17). By the power of the Holy Spirit, Christian learn to embody this uncreated light and love, what this meditation calls "Deep Light" and "Deep Love."

Is it always, or usually, clear to you which is the wisest course of action in a complex situation? How then does walking in the way of wisdom sometimes involve a kind of walking in intellectual darkness?

CHAPTER 5

The One Who Is has no preference or prejudice
    concerning secondary things.
So, wise shepherds also treat secondary matters
    as truly and really secondary in importance.
This allows concentration on what is truly significant.

As the creative Eternal Love and Uncreated Light
    of the One Who Is and Will Be,
        the Word empties itself of overt power.

Word and Spirit work invisibly in Deep Light,
    creating all things in the silence of hidden power,
        uniting Heaven and Earth in Deep Love.

Wise shepherds take note of the greatness
    of hidden influence.
Wise shepherds are never anxious
    to be seen at work.
Wise shepherds focus on serving others.
Then, success comes to everyone.

Be filled with the Spirit; it produces deep wisdom—
    mere talk of wisdom produces little progress.
It is better to remain silent and centered
    on the mystery of uncreated Love and Light.

How many are your works, O Lord! In wisdom you made them all; . . . When you send your Spirit, they are created, and you renew the face of the earth.
(Psalm 104:24, 30 [NIV])

Concentrate on the Most Important Things

It is easy to lose perspective and become overly attached to secondary things. For the Taoist and Christian, it is important to detach ourselves from what is secondary and focus on truly important things. A life lived in accordance with the Way is lived with wise understanding and wise priorities.

Jesus says, "Seek first the kingdom of God and his righteousness and all these things will be added unto you as well" (Matthew 6:33). Our first priority should be God. This is especially important for leaders. Leadership inevitably involves the external search for success. In order to achieve a proper sense of priorities, Christ-Followers who are also leaders must learn to detach from the urgent in meditation and prayer in order to be properly attuned to the Word. This is the work of the Spirit of Christ empowering believers to live in the manner of Christ.

What are the real priorities of your life? Are your priorities the same as those taught by the Bible? What does it mean to you to remain silently centered in "Uncreated Love and Light?" How would it change your life if you learned to appreciate the necessity of silence and waiting?

CHAPTER 6

Before time, the Spirit brooded upon waters of chaos.
The Spirit is called "the Creator Spirit"
   because it gave birth
      to the heavens and earth,
         the visible and the invisible.

The Spirit is everywhere
   with the One Who Is and the Word
      in Uncreated Light and Eternal Love.

The Spirit is like mist at the base of a great waterfall—
   barely discerned, invisible, yet always present.
The Spirit cannot be exhausted;
   it is never used up however much it is expended.
The wise shepherd allows the Spirit
   to inspire and guide in heated circumstances.

Like a gentle rain, the Spirit comes upon those who wait.
Then, wise action follows like new grass in the spring.

In silence, let the Creator Spirit gently fill you.
This is the Way of Deep Light.

IN THE BEGINNING GOD CREATED THE HEAVENS AND THE EARTH.
THE EARTH WAS WITHOUT FORM, AND VOID; AND DARKNESS *WAS* ON
THE FACE OF THE DEEP. AND THE SPIRIT OF GOD WAS HOVERING
OVER THE FACE OF THE WATERS.
(Genesis 1:1–2 [NKJV])

Be Filled with the Creator Spirit

For the Taoist, the foundation of heaven and earth is the Tao.
Like the womb, it is the starting place of life. Like a great valley, it
is a source of vegetation and growth. Like a spring, it is the fount
of life giving water. Heaven and earth emerge from this source.
One who lives in accordance with the Way finds the source of wise
living.

For the Christ-Follower, the Triune God is the great source of
heaven and earth, "of all things visible and invisible," as the Nicene
Creed puts it. The Word is the rational principle of creation:
the order we perceive reflects the divine order God implanted in
Creation by his Word. The Spirit is the power of God's love creating
as it broods over chaos. A Christ-Follower who lives according to
the Word is filled with the Spirit of God. Such a Christ-Follower
is empowered by the Spirit to live wisely and well—a quality he or
she imparts to others.

People struggle through all or portions of life. If the
Word, being God, rules without struggle by the power of the
God's Spirit, why do we struggle so in our daily lives?

Chapter 7

The One Who Is and Will Be
    is from everlasting to everlasting,
        and the earth has existed for age upon age.

Present by Divine Love for all things,
    the One Who Is created all things in Deep Light,
        and the Word sustains all things
            in Deep Love like a nursing mother.

Serving others, the wise person detaches his or her ego
    from bondage to created things.

The wise leader serves humbly,
    coming to a place of authority
        by the power of the Spirit.

Therefore, the wise are united
    with all things in Uncreated Deep Love
        and perceive all things
            by Uncreated Deep Light.

Wise persons reject selfish, self-centered ambition,
    yet are perfectly fulfilled and blessed in all they do.

This is the secret wisdom and power
    of uncreated Deep Light and Love.

Do not push yourself forward at court or take your stand where the great assemble; for it is better to be told, "Come up here" than to be moved down to make room for a nobleman.
(Proverbs 25:6–7 [REV])

Humbly Serve Deep Light and Deep Love

The Tao is the ground of all things. The Tao does not exist for itself. It exists for the creation of which it is the inexhaustible source. The Way is ultimately a servant, nurturing the creation. In Taoism, the humble sage is like the Tao; he or she unassumingly serves the needs of others and so finds fulfillment.

In Christianity, God is the eternal and inexhaustible source of all things. Christianity contains the same kind of teaching as the Tao. Jesus says, "Whoever tries to keep his life (his egocentric desires) will lose it, and whoever loses his life (his egocentric desires) will preserve it" (Luke 17:33). A person who devotes himself or herself to humble service finds eternal life in the process. United with divine, sacrificial love, what this adaptation calls "Deep Love," such a person finds the deepest self-fulfillment and can act as a vehicle for God's love in the lives of others.

What does it mean for a Christian to "detach the ego" from created things? In what way is your ego "attached" to created things and how does that keep you from realizing your potential as a human being and as a Christian leader?

CHAPTER 8

Water moves naturally toward low places.
Water serves the Creation—
    bringing new life, nurturing and
        benefiting all things.

The best human beings walk in the Way
    as water flows along the rocky bed
        of a mountain stream.

A wise person remembers these truths:

    Stay close to the earth in humility.
    Love the wisdom of the Word and the Way.
    Love creation with Deep Love.
    Love others with Deep Love.
    Love just and orderly management.
    Love timeliness in word and deed.
    Handle business with diligent competence.

Do not be driven by a spirit of competition,
    but by the Spirit of Love and Light.

People like this are beyond criticism.

Everyone who drinks this water will be thirsty again, but whoever drinks of the water I give him will never thirst. Indeed, the water I give him will become in him a spring of living water, welling up into eternal life.
(John 4:13–14 [NIV])

Be Willing to Seek the Lowly Places

Jesus speaks of water as a metaphor for the life-giving power of the Spirit (John 4:13–14). The *Tao Te Ching* uses the simile of water for the character of the virtuous person. Water gives life. By nature, water seeks the lowest spot. The best people mirror these characteristics of water. Wise people are not afraid to find meaning in humble servanthood.

Wise people love the earth and humble connection with the earth. This involves deep love of people, faithfulness in personal relations, orderliness, and attention to detail. As the Word Incarnate served in lowliness and humility, so those who follow the Way of the Word live quietly and competently. Wise people seek simplicity and recognize that, in accepting ourselves as God made us, we find peace. In leadership, this attitude protects a leader from pride and overreaching. Such people are a source of life-giving love and wisdom to others.

Do you agree that wise people are like water, seeking low places of service? How would your life change if serving others was your primary goal in life?

CHAPTER 9

The cup of life was given by the One Who Is
    to fill with good things.
Yet, filling the cup of life to overflowing is unwise
    and involves wastefulness.

Excessive material wealth and many possessions
    are difficult to preserve and maintain.
Those who are proud due to excessive honor,
    wealth, or power often grasp too much
        and lose everything.

A pocketknife sharpened too far
    quickly breaks or becomes dull.

Excessive striving leads to anxiety and stress.

Rest is needed.
Childlike simplicity is needed.

This is the way of the wise leader: accomplish a work,
    and then humbly withdraw and go on
        to whatever task comes next.

This is the way of the wise shepherd.

FOR TO THE ONE WHO PLEASES HIM, GOD GIVES WISDOM AND
KNOWLEDGE AND JOY; BUT TO THE SINNER HE GIVES THE TASK OF
GATHERING AND HEAPING, ONLY GIVE TO THE ONE WHO PLEASES
GOD. THIS ALSO IS VANITY AND A CHASING AFTER WIND.
(Ecclesiastes 2:26 [NRSV])

Do not Attempt Too Much

First Peter 5:5 says, "All of you, clothe yourselves with humility
toward one another, because, God opposes the proud but gives grace
to the humble." Pride is one of the seven deadly sins, indeed the
deadliest of all. "The Lord detests the proud of heart" (Proverbs
16:5). Pride is serious because it always results in overreaching.

The *Tao Te Ching* teaches that it is a mistake to fill one's life with
prideful, personal striving. Pride attempts to accomplish too much.
It is also a mistake to try to perform at the highest level for too
long. As the *Tao Te Ching* puts it, a knife sharpened to too sharp an
edge quickly dulls. Appropriate labor, accomplishment, withdrawal,
and rest are central to successful living. Since leaders often strive for
accomplishment and success, it is particularly important for them
to learn the value of respecting human limits. Otherwise, leaders
put themselves in a position of overreaching and failure.

*Have you ever known a person who attempted to grab too much or undertake too
much? Was the result like the result that the Tao Te Ching predicts? How does a
person avoid prideful overreaching in his or her life?*

CHAPTER 10

Can you center yourself in the Creator Spirit?
Can you embrace Eternal Light and Eternal Love?
Can you meditate until distractions depart?

Can you quietly center your spirit in the Eternal
    until you develop childlike simplicity?
Can you allow the Spirit to cleanse your spirit
    so you are born anew by Deep Love?
Can you love people and lead them
    without manipulation or force?
Can you be content, allowing the Eternal to
    create, rule, give, and take away?
Can you walk in perplexing darkness
    by the Deep Light of the Word,
        not trusting your own understanding?

Can you:

> Give birth and nourish all things in Deep Love?
> Act trusting the One Who Is?
> Lead without conflict, violence, or force?

If you can, you possess the virtue of the Way.

LET THE LITTLE CHILDREN COME UNTO ME AND DO NOT STOP
THEM, FOR IT IS TO SUCH AS THESE THAT THE KINGDOM OF GOD
BELONGS. TRULY, I TELL YOU, WHOEVER DOES NOT RECEIVE THE
KINGDOM OF GOD AS A LITTLE CHILD WILL NEVER ENTER IT.
(Luke 18:16–17 [NRSV])

Give Childlike Attention to the One Who Is

In Mark we read, "Very early in the morning, while it was
still dark, Jesus got up, left the house and went off to a solitary
place, where he prayed" (Mark 1:35). The ability to pray, quietly
center oneself, and embrace the Way with childlike simplicity is an
important characteristic of the wise life. Jesus practiced the same
childlike simplicity he preached.

Jesus could say, like the Psalmist, "I have stilled and quieted
my soul, like a weaned child with its mother, like a weaned child is
my soul within me" (Psalm 131:2). This is not a withdrawal into
private religious experience, but a centering in, speaking with, and
listening to God. Where this kind of prayer is practiced, human
beings develop the ability to see reality clearly, love others, and serve
their deepest interests in everyday life. Such a person is filled with
hope, not because of striving, but in reliance on God.

*Jesus says that we must become like a child and the Tao agrees. Why does wisdom
require us to adopt an attitude of childlike attention toward reality? How does
one create and lead without grasping and using force? Is this realistic?*

CHAPTER 11

Many spokes join at the center of a wheel,
    but the wheel rotates around
        the stillness of its center.

The potter molds clay into a cup,
    but it is the emptiness inside the cup
        upon which utility depends.

The carpenter builds a house with walls,
    but within the rooms of the home
        an owner dwells.

What already exists is useful,
    but what does not yet exist is more useful.
What is and what will be are both
    the work of the One Who Is and Will Be.

The faithful and wise shepherd
    considers what is and what is yet to come,
        remains centered in the Word, and
            follows the Way.

MOSES SAID TO GOD, "SUPPOSE I GO TO THE ISRAELITES AND SAY
TO THEM, 'THE GOD OF YOUR FATHERS HAS SENT ME TO YOU,'
AND THEY ASK ME, 'WHAT IS HIS NAME?' THEN WHAT SHALL I TELL
THEM?" GOD SAID TO MOSES, "I AM WHO I AM. THIS IS WHAT YOU
ARE TO SAY TO THE ISRAELITES: 'I AM HAS SENT ME TO YOU.' "
(Exodus 3:13-14 [NIV])

Remember the Importance of Potential

Those of us who grew up in Western Culture naturally think
of walls as central to the room, the form of the pot as central to
the pot, the molding of the window as central to the window. Is
this the deepest truth? It is the stillness at the center around which
a wheel circulates; it is the emptiness at the center of a pot that
makes it useful; it is the emptiness within the walls of the house in
which we live.

In the Old Testament, God shares with Moses a name, which
can be translated, "I Am that I Am" or "I Will Be What I Will
Be" (Exodus 3:14). This name points to God as the inexhaustible
source of potentiality and being. In stillness and prayer, we become
aware of and connected to this inexhaustible source of being. In
being connected to the One Who Is and Will Be, we connect with
the source of all creativity and transformation.

Most people use only a small part of their potential.
What does it mean to consider not just what is but also what is
not in taking action? How would you change if you pondered what
is not present in your life and character in making decisions?

CHAPTER 12

Too much color confuses the gazing eye.
Too much sound inhibits the hearing ear.
Too many spices dull the tasting palate.
Too many meaningless activities
    make one hasty and unstable in action.
Too much wealth results in greediness.
For this reason, the wise person
    practices moderation.

In quiet thought and balanced action,
    the wise person rejects the superficial,
        seeking Reality beneath appearances.

A heart centered in the Word is trustworthy—
    understanding the deeply Real and True,
        perceiving in the depths of the heart
            the harmony of Goodness and Beauty.

I DID NOT RESTRAIN MYSELF FROM ANY JOY. I EVEN FOUND GREAT
PLEASURE IN HARD WORK, AN ADDITIONAL REWARD FOR ALL MY
LABORS. BUT AS I LOOKED AT EVERYTHING I HAD WORKED SO HARD
TO ACCOMPLISH, IT WAS ALL SO MEANINGLESS. IT WAS LIKE CHASING
THE WIND. THERE WAS NOTHING REALLY WORTHWHILE ANYWHERE.
(Ecclesiastes 2:10–11 [NLT])

Ponder the Essential; Discern the Superficial

We live in an age of over-stimulation. We constantly view
television and movies. We eat well-cooked and well-spiced meals.
We listen to music and talk radio wherever we go. We engage in
endless activities. We have too little time to be still and listen.

Yet, simplicity and meditation are essential to the wise life. "Be
still and know that I am God," says the Psalmist (Psalm 46:10).
Jesus often went to a solitary place to listen to the Father (Luke
4:42). In order to understand the deepest and most important
mysteries of life, we must develop the ability to cut ourselves off
from the frenetic sights, sounds, and constant activity of superficial
living. We must learn to listen to the still small voice of God, for
the deepest mysteries of life and creation are revealed in stillness
and in silence.

*Can you think of a time in your life when you failed to keep centered and acted
superficially or unwisely? Can you think of situations in which a person you
know did something superficial because he or she failed to look deeply into reality?*

CHAPTER 13

The wise leader is apprehensive about success and failure.
    Both great success and painful failure
        draw one away from the quiet Center.

The wise shepherd takes trouble and opposition seriously,
    remembering that success is as dangerous as failure.

Excessive success results in self confident pride—
    fear it even more than failure.

In life and death, embrace the One Who Is.
Trust the Deep Love of the Eternal;
    remain tranquil in the Way—it brings wisdom.

Face opposition and trouble without fear.
Facing trouble develops courage.

A person who is filled with Deep Light
    senses his or her False Self.
A person who is filled with Deep Love
    loves all people and things, rejecting the False Self.

A person who is trustworthy in all things
    receives the Peace of Heaven.

Two things I ask of you: . . . Remove far from me falsehood
and lying; give me neither poverty nor riches, feed me with
the food that I need, or I shall be full, and deny you, and
say, "Who is the Lord?" or, I shall be poor, and steal, and
profane the name of my God.

(Proverbs 30:7–9 [NRSV])

Avoid the Danger of Too Much Success

We are elated by success and public praise and depressed by
opposition, criticism, and failure. Our egos, our sense of self, are
too bound up in what we have and what we do. On the other hand,
the *Tao Te Ching* and teachings of Christ urge us to view success and
failure as secondary. Who we *are* and what kind of person we *are
becoming* are more important than anything else.

If we are humbly serving others in love, then success and
failure are relatively unimportant. Those who embody this servant
spirit embody the Spirit of the One who "came to serve, not to be
served" (Matthew 20:28). In order to serve others with this spirit,
we must overcome our own ego-driven desires. We must center
ourselves in Christ. When we become this kind of servant leader,
we are servants of the Way.

*Everyone knows that failure is dangerous. Why is success as
dangerous as failure? Can you think of a time when you failed,
yet that failure helped you achieve later success?*

CHAPTER 14

The Way is a lighted path in every kind of darkness.
The Way is not discerned with human eyes;
 even in darkness it is discerned in Deep Light.
Deep Wisdom is not heard with human ears.
Only the eternal Word reveals it.

We cannot force a revelation.
Infinite, Boundless, Almighty, and Majestic:
 descriptions of the One Who Is fall short.
Only the Word reveals the One Who Is and Will Be.

Mysterious, beyond human comprehension,
 present at the creation in divine light,
  humble and transparent in self-giving love,
   the Creator Spirit reveals the Word.

Follow the Way of the One Who Is and Will Be;
 you will not find an end to the Way of the Word.

Trust the One Who Is.
Embody the Word.
Follow the Way.
Patiently become wise.

This is the essence of the Way.

THE PEOPLE THAT WALKED IN DARKNESS HAVE SEEN
A GREAT LIGHT; ON THOSE WHO LIVED IN A LAND AS DARK AS
DEATH A LIGHT HAS DAWNED.
(Isaiah 9:2 [REV])

Embrace the Mystery of the Eternal Way

The Way cannot be seen with our eyes or heard with our ears. Yet, it is the source of true guidance. God cannot be seen with human eyes or heard with human ears, yet God is the source of true guidance and wisdom for living. This is true even in dark and difficult times.

We can only know the deepest truths by the Spirit. As Paul said, "'No eye has seen, no ear has heard, no mind has conceived what God has prepared for those who love him'—but God has revealed it to us by his Spirit. The Spirit searches all things, even the deep things of God" (I Corinthians 2:8–10). As we practice humble listening and obedience to the silent Word, we sense the light of God's secret, hidden wisdom leading us. This requires patience, trust, study, and listening. As we are filled by the Spirit of Christ, the One Who Is reveals the proper course, even when current circumstances seem to block out the light and we can barely find our way forward.

Life is complex and sometimes difficult. The Way of Wisdom is often dark, and the will of the Word is often not apparent. How do we hear God speaking in silence and in times of darkness when seeking solutions to difficult problems? Why is waiting so important in this process of listening and seeking solutions?

Chapter 15

Wise shepherds penetrate difficult and confusing matters,
    knowing the mystery of discerning deep things.
The character of a wise leader is deep, mystifying,
    and cannot be fully described.
Wise shepherds are cautious,
    like one crossing an icy mountain stream.
Wise shepherds are concerned,
    like one surrounded by aggressive enemies.
Wise shepherds are considerate,
    like an ambassador to a hostile land.
Wise shepherds are flexible,
    like a young tree bent by a large hurricane.
Wise shepherds are broad-minded,
    like a wide and fertile valley.
Wise shepherds are genuine and gentle,
    like a dove feeding in a winter wheat field.
Wise shepherds remain motionless
    until the best course of action is revealed.
Wise shepherds act with energy
    when the best course is revealed.
Wise shepherds are not always striving anxiously,
    wearing themselves out in ceaseless,
        meaningless activity.

It is the glory of God to conceal a matter;
to search out a matter is the glory of kings.
As the heavens are high and the earth is deep,
so the hearts of kings are unsearchable.
(Proverbs 25:2–3 [NIV])

Discern the Hidden Reality of Things

Life is complicated. We face situations in which wise and foolish courses of action are not easily distinguished. Human beings need self-control, which involves the ability to remain thoughtfully calm until the wise time to act arrives. The essential characteristics of the prudent person are, therefore, discernment, flexibility, caution, genuiness, good manners, and lack of guile. This allows us to accurately size up people and situations.

Over and over again, Scripture says Jesus "knew" what was in the hearts of those who opposed him (See, Matthew 12:15; Luke 6:8). Yet, he was without guile. One cannot imagine Jesus scheming. He never displayed rashness. Jesus was never rude, even when pressured. Christ-Followers need the virtue of wise discernment. They should require discernment and other virtues in their leaders, especially in those who shepherd our spiritual lives. Specifically, a wise leader acts carefully, doing what is prudent, understanding that complicated problems are seldom easily solved.

Why is penetrating reason and caution so important in a wise leader? Do you find it hard to remain quiet while waiting for God to act? Why is boldness a difficult virtue to embody wisely?

CHAPTER 16

Empty your mind of trivial, superficial thoughts.
Maintain a quiet, tranquil, and peaceful heart.
With your physical eye, observe reality.
With the inner eye, contemplate its meaning.
Perceive the deeply true and real in every situation.
You will find the path of Deep Light.

All things come into being, mature, and then disintegrate.
All things grow, wither, and then die.
All things return to their beginning.
When things return to their source, there is quiet,
    as created things come to their appointed end.

A person who cannot understand the Way
    acts rashly in a crisis—disaster results.

A person who understands the Way
    acts with Deep Love for all things,
        giving to each as it deserves—
            success results.

Being one with the Word, a person follows the Way.
Following the Way, one finds the Kingdom of Heaven.

One who finds the Kingdom of Heaven does not fear death.

HELP ME UNDERSTAND THE MEANING OF YOUR COMMANDMENTS,
AND I WILL MEDITATE ON YOUR WONDERFUL DEEDS.
(Psalm 119:26-28 [NLT]).

Attain the Calm of True Wisdom

We live in an impulsive and impatient culture. We also live in a culture that is faddish. Wise living and wise leadership require that we be patiently observant. In order for our perceptions to be accurate, observation must be supplemented by meditation. In particular, it is important to consider in every situation what is truly meaningful and what is of passing importance. We need to treat people and eternal things as most important and treat created things as secondary. When we do this, we become wise.

Paul puts it this way, "Then we will no longer be infants, tossed back and forth by the waves, and blown here and there by every wind of teaching and by the cunning and craftiness of men in their deceitful scheming. Instead, speaking the truth in love, we will in all things grow up into him who is the Head, that is, Christ" (Ephesians 4:14–15). When we understand both the truth in a situation and what can and cannot be done in love, we are on the way to true wisdom.

What does it mean to you for a person to "observe with the outer eye and contemplate with the inner eye?" Why is rashness such a disaster for a leader?

CHAPTER 17

Followers hardly perceive the best shepherds exist.
Next are shepherds who inspire admiration and praise.
Lower still are shepherds who inspire dread and fear.
The worst shepherds are loathed and despised.

If you don't trust people, they become untrustworthy.

Value the power of words.
The best words point to Reality.
The worst words distort Reality.
So, use words sparingly to convey Truth.

When Words reflect Reality, the correct path can be
     seen and therefore chosen.

Wise leaders never manipulate;
     they are gentle and truthful shepherds.

When a wise leader's task is accomplished, people say,

                    "We did it, ourselves!"

So, wise shepherds empower others.

You know that among the Gentiles the recognized rulers
lord it over their subjects and the great make their
authority felt. It shall not be so among you; among you,
whoever wants to be great must be your servant, and
whoever wants to be first must be the slave of all.
(Mark 10:42–45 [REV])

Develop the True Simplicity of a Leader

We want leaders who are visible, active, and powerful. We want leaders to act boldly to solve business, community, local, and national problems. Too often, pride, desire, and greed drive such leaders to overstep appropriate boundaries.

The Way teaches that the best leaders are those who serve humbly. Jesus says, "If anyone wants to be first, he must be the very last, and the servant of all" (Mark 9:35). Such leaders are servant/shepherds who empower followers. Those they lead have a sense of accomplishment and personal growth. This meets a deep human need to feel competent to solve the ordinary problems of life. In the end, leaders who empower others build up those they lead and solve problems in the process. Leaders who provide this kind of leadership provide the most important leadership of all.

The Tao suggests that leaders should remain hidden. Why? How can a leader be both visible and active in helping a group achieve an objective and at the same time "hidden?" Can leaders resolve the paradox caused the necessity of both visibility and hiddenness in exercising leadership?

CHAPTER 18

When the Way is deserted by a culture,
    people merely talk about charity and righteousness.
When excessive intellectualism arises,
    people talk about the good but avoid right action.

When Deep Love is absent and character decays,
    people merely talk about brotherly love.
Where there is Deep Love and people attain virtue,
    there is no need for mindless chatter.

When a country falls into chaos through foolishness,
    politicians talk constantly about love of country.
Where there is love of family, city, and nation,
    there is little need for patriotic talk.

Character is better than talking.
Virtue is more important than fine speeches.

[I]N THE LAST DAYS THERE WILL BE VERY DIFFICULT TIMES. FOR
PEOPLE WILL LOVE ONLY THEMSELVES AND THEIR MONEY. THEY
WILL BE BOASTFUL AND PROUD, SCOFFING AT GOD, DISOBEDIENT TO
THEIR PARENTS, AND UNGRATEFUL. THEY WILL CONSIDER NOTHING
SACRED. THEY WILL BE UNLOVING AND UNFORGIVING; THEY WILL
SLANDER OTHERS AND HAVE NO SELF-CONTROL. THEY WILL BE
CRUEL AND HATE WHAT IS GOOD . . . YOU MUST STAY AWAY FROM
PEOPLE LIKE THAT!
(2 Timothy 3:1-5 [NLT])

Character Is More Important than Talk

Lao Tzu suggests that there is an order to the Way: First, personal
virtue, then family virtue, then community virtue, then national
virtue. When a matter becomes a topic of public debate, there is
often a problem deeper than the debate. The debate is a symptom
of the problem. So, when people begin to talk about the need to
maintain morals, it may be that morals are already corrupt.

When people begin to talk about family values, the family may
already be in trouble. When politicians begin to extol the virtue of
patriotism, there may already be a lack of true patriotism. Where
there is love and virtue, there is no need to talk. The message seems
to be, "Talk is cheap; love and virtue require more than talk."

Why do people talk about virtue in times of social decay?
Does this help you to understand some of the reasons for
contemporary talk about the virtues in public life?

CHAPTER 19

Wise persons should not seek to be acclaimed as wise—
     so abandon false wisdom and your False Self.

Wise shepherds do not superficially care for others,
          saying and doing only what gives a good name.
Wise leaders care deeply for others with Deep Love,
          and then followers return to Way.

Abandon professional striving and unrestrained greed,
          and there will be very little opportunity
                    for thieves and robbers.

          Keep to the Way.
          Seek Deep Light.
          Embody Deep Love.
          Manifest Simplicity of Life.
          Resist Selfishness.

This is the path of Deep Light.

FOR THE MESSAGE OF THE CROSS IS FOOLISHNESS TO THOSE WHO
ARE PERISHING, BUT TO US WHO ARE BEING SAVED IT IS THE POWER
OF GOD. FOR IT IS WRITTEN, "I WILL DESTROY THE WISDOM
OF THE WISE; THE INTELLIGENCE OF THE INTELLIGENT I WILL
FRUSTRATE."
(1 Corinthians 1:18–19 [NIV])

Manifest Simplicity and Deep Caring

In a culture that worships success and values the exterior over
the interior of a person, the Way asks us to focus on what cannot
be seen. It is not important for others to know we are wise. It is
important to be wise. It is not important that we superficially love
others to make a reputation. We must truly and deeply love others
in order to make a difference in their lives.

This chapter of the *Tao Te Ching* contains one of its clearest
teachings on the character of the wise person: "Manifest plainness,
embrace simplicity, reduce selfishness, have few desires." Deep Love
comes as we control our self-love and become simple. Contemporary,
narcissistic leaders seldom meet these requirements. Such leaders
are too busy meeting their own ego needs to care for or empower
others. The message of Jesus is hidden from such leaders.

*Do the virtues of plainness, simplicity, unselfishness, and patience appeal to
you? How would your life be different if it were characterized by plainness,
selflessness, and simplicity? What keeps you from achieving these virtues?*

CHAPTER 20

Abandon superficial understanding;
   and, the wisdom of Deep Light will come.
What is the essential difference
   between yes and no?
What is the essential distinction
   between good and evil?
What is the essential line of separation
   between wise and foolish behavior?

The wise accept uncertainty with patience.
Still the wise fear what common people fear—
   as they meditate on the Word, seeking the Way.

The multitude eats, drinks, and is merry;
   wise people consider and are still.
The multitude strives for possessions;
   wise people are content with enough.
The multitude is satisfied with common opinion;
   wise people seek the wisdom of Deep Light.

Ordinary people appear to understand all things.
Wise people may appear unable to understand anything,
   as they patiently gaze deeply into Reality,
     awaiting a revelation of the Way.
This is the character of the Way:
   it awaits Deep Light speaking in Deep Love.

To be wise you must first have reverence for the Lord. If you know the Holy One, you will have understanding.
(Proverbs 9:10 [TEV])

Renounce Superficial Wisdom

In daily life, we rely upon "discursive intelligence" in making decisions. We make distinctions. We discuss and argue. We make our point. We look at business situations with an eye to profit. In politics, we count the votes. In many ways, discursive intelligence determines our success or failure. From the perspective of eternity, this type of intelligence, useful as it is, is secondary. A more important kind of understanding comes from God.

In First Corinthians, Paul speaks of the secret, hidden wisdom of God (See 1 Corinthians 2:7). This deeper wisdom involves an appreciation of the moral and spiritual aspects of reality as well as understanding "the way the world works." From the perspective of those trapped in mere worldly shrewdness, this deeper wisdom actually appears foolish, but it is the ground of true wisdom. This kind of understanding comes only from God, and begins as we learn to revere and worship God.

*In your mind, what kinds of wisdom are superficial
(mere shrewdness or cunning) and what kinds of wisdom are deep
and profound? What does it mean to look into events and situations and
seek the Deep Light and Deep Love in a person or problem?*

CHAPTER 21

Deep Light reveals the Way.
Deep Love characterizes the Way.
Virtue comes from following the Way.

Followers of the Way seek the Deep Light—
　　even as they walk a dark and dangerous path.
The Path of Wisdom is often difficult and narrow—
　　still the wise hold to the Way.
Subtle and difficult to grasp, yet clearly manifested,
　　hidden and mysterious, yet plainly revealed,
　　　　the Word lights the Way of the wise.

The light-giving power of the Word is genuine.
In the Word, the order of all things is found.
Have faith in the Word.

The wise seek the Word—the source of all things.
　　This is the beginning of the journey of wisdom.

AGAIN JESUS SPOKE TO THEM, SAYING, "I AM THE LIGHT OF THE
WORLD. WHOEVER FOLLOWS ME WILL NEVER WALK IN DARKNESS
BUT WILL HAVE THE LIGHT OF LIFE."
(John 8:12 [NRSV])

Follow the Path of Deep Light

According to the *Tao Te Ching*, virtue comes from following the
Tao and the Tao alone. For Christianity, the deepest wisdom comes
from following the revelation of the Word in Christ and the Way
of life this revelation entails. This path can seem dark and difficult,
but its end is the deepest possible wisdom.

Scripture says, "The people walking in darkness have seen a
great light; on those living in the land of the shadow of death a
light has dawned" (Isaiah 9:2). Christianity affirms that God is
transcendent and therefore ultimately unknowable in the totality
of the divine being. There is a "darkness" in the search for God's
will. Yet, Christianity also affirms that God is Light, ultimately
rational and the unfathomable ground of reason and truth. Those
who seek this Eternal Light will not be disappointed, however dark
the immediate path. Christ-Followers see in Jesus the light of God's
presence in human form. By following Christ, we walk in the light
even when the immediate path is dark.

What makes the way of wisdom so difficult? When has your path been dark?
Where did you look for guidance? Does wise leadership sometimes have to "walk
a dark and dangerous path" while seeking a wise course of action?

CHAPTER 22

Followers of the Way accept the inevitable:

> The way to become straight involves bending.
> The way to find fulfillment involves being poured out.
> The way to eternal youth involves becoming old.
> The path to eternal life involves death of the False Self.

Wise leaders do not justify themselves,
>   and so are recognized by others.
Wise shepherds are not proud or self-exalted,
>   and so given credit by those they serve.
Wise leaders do not strive beyond proper limits,
>   and so the world cannot overcome them.
Wise shepherds do not boast,
>   and so are lifted up.
Wise leaders are not proud,
>   and so worthy of being exalted.

If you want to become truly whole and filled with joy,
>   accept suffering for the sake of Deep Love.

If you follow these words, you follow the Path of Life.

THEN JESUS SAID TO HIS DISCIPLES, "IF ANYONE WOULD COME
AFTER ME, HE MUST DENY HIMSELF AND TAKE UP HIS CROSS AND
FOLLOW ME."
(Matthew 16:24 [NIV])

Accept the Paradox of the Way

The world can be improved, but it cannot be perfected. Humble people understand their own limits and the limits of others. Wise people are not too proud to yield their personal rights and privileges for the common good. The wise do not attempt things beyond their power to accomplish. They are willing to embrace the loss of selfish desire to help others.

For Christ-Followers, the deepest truth is embodied by Christ on the Cross. So, wise leaders are not afraid to deny themselves on behalf of those they lead. Wise love is not afraid to suffer for the beloved. Paradoxically, in doing this, wise believers connect with the deepest possible source of power—the power of Suffering Love, what scholars call, "Cruciform Love". This is the love of God that lies at the center of God's being. Leaders will only demonstrate self restraint if they embody the sacrificial, self-giving love of the Cross in their ordinary, day to day lives. There is no other path to truly transformational leadership.

The Tao Te Ching teaches that it is better to yield, to bend, to deny your own desires rather than struggle for victory. In what kinds of situations do you find this advice is helpful? In what kind of situations do you find this advice most difficult to apply?

CHAPTER 23

A violent windstorm passes quickly,
    yet fells the tallest trees with invisible power.
A fierce thunderstorm lasts a short while,
    yet nurtures the earth with drops of water.
A great snowstorm melts with the coming spring,
    yet nourishes the valley below.
Creation is silent as the darkest night,
    yet speaks with the eloquence of Deep Light.

One who follows the Way is united with the Word.
One who is united with the Word finds virtue in the Way.
One who takes up his or her Cross, finds Eternal Life.
This is the Way of Wisdom.

One who abandons the Way leaves the Path of Life.
This is the Path of Foolishness.

One who follows the Way, the Word will not abandon.

Faith in others breeds faith in the one believed.
Distrust in others breeds distrust the one doubted.
Therefore, show trust toward others if possible.
You will nourish trust in others around you.

THE HEAVENS DECLARE THE GLORY OF GOD, AND THE SKY ABOVE
PROCLAIMS HIS HANDIWORK. DAY TO DAY POURS OUT SPEECH AND
NIGHT TO NIGHT REVEALS KNOWLEDGE. THERE IS NO SPEECH, NOR
ARE THERE WORDS, WHOSE VOICE IS NOT HEARD.
(Psalm 19:1–4 [ESV])

Unite With the Word; Follow the Way

The Word speaking in creation is "silent," yet it is the ground of creation's intelligibility. In science, humans use mathematics to describe our limited understanding of reality. In the realm of morals and the spirit, human languages illuminate our partial understanding of a divine order that transcends words. The Word is the Uncreated Wisdom of God—wisdom beyond human expression.

Christ-Followers seek both created and uncreated wisdom in reaching decisions. Christians need an understanding of the world and the way it works. Christians also need a spiritual understanding of spiritual things to live wisely. In seeking the "silent Word of God," people of the Way are empowered to discern the deepest things of all. This silent listening meditates on the Word and on his creation. As Christians ponder the silent speech of God, the Spirit speaks to the heart, and believers are united with the wisdom of Christ.

What does it mean to live a life characterized by unity with the Word and faithfulness to the Way? The Tao Te Ching teaches that those who trust others are trusted and those who do not trust others are not trusted. Do you agree? Why or why not?

CHAPTER 24

One who grasps beyond proper limits
  is always off balance and in danger of slipping.
One who by force drives beyond proper limits
  makes little if any progress.
One who aggressively seeks public acclaim
  quickly fades from the popular mind.

Self-promoters have no enduring fame.
Those who boast diminish their accomplishments.
Striving beyond created limits brings disaster.
Compared to the Way, these actions are unworthy.

Followers of the Way,
  live humbly within human limitations,
    content to serve others.

Therefore, live simply as a child of the Word.

BLESSED ARE THE POOR IN SPIRIT; THE KINGDOM OF HEAVEN
IS THEIRS. BLESSED ARE THE SORROWFUL; THEY SHALL FIND
CONSOLATION. BLESSED ARE THE GENTLE, FOR THEY SHALL HAVE
THE EARTH FOR THEIR POSSESSION.
(Matthew 5:3–5 [REV])

Be Blessed in Showing Humility

Balance is important to practitioners of Tai Chi (a Chinese form of Yoga). The person who is always striving to do more or accomplish more is usually spiritually or morally off balance. They are always in danger of tripping.

Those who follow the Way live within human limitations. Thus, the *Tao Te Ching* and Christian faith advise a wise balance in life. This is the wisdom of the Beatitudes, when they teach us, "Blessed are the poor in spirit, for theirs is the kingdom of heaven" (Matthew 5:3) and "Blessed are the meek, for they will inherit the earth" (Matthew 5:5). Humility and meekness breed patient, well-balanced living. Well-balanced people have no need of arrogance, violence, self-promotion, or other strategies of the false self. They are content to be themselves. They possess spiritual and moral balance. Love of God and others shines through their lives.

*Can you describe a time when you were seeking too hard to gain
something and ended up off balance and missing an opportunity?
What did it feel like then and later? Can you think of a time when you
felt balanced and free while trying to achieve something? What did that
experience feel like then and later? What was the difference?*

Chapter 25

Before the created order existed,
    when there was chaos on the face of the deep,
        Uncreated Light dwelt in Uncreated Love.

The Word dwells everywhere.
Dwelling everywhere,
    the Word operates everywhere
        by the silent power of the Spirit.

Vast is the One Who Is.
Vast is the Way.
Vast is the Creation.
Vast of spirit are those created in the image of the Word.

There is peace in Heaven and Earth when:

        Humanity follows the way of Creation.
        Creation follows the Way.
        The Way springs from the Word.
        The Word is begotten of the One Who Is.

There is order when all things are
    properly related to the One Who Is.

THE WORLD AND ALL THAT IS IN IT BELONG TO THE LORD; THE
EARTH AND ALL WHO LIVE ON IT ARE HIS. HE BUILT IT ON THE DEEP
WATERS BENEATH THE EARTH AND LAID ITS FOUNDATIONS IN THE
OCEAN DEPTHS.
(Psalm 24:1–2 [TEV])

Follow the Way of Creation

In Taoism, before creation the Tao existed as a formless
potentiality. It is the mother of all things. For Christianity, the
Word existed before creation as the Only-Begotten Divine Light
of God. What Taoism and Christianity have in common is the
notion that there is an eternal Tao (Way or Word), which operates
everywhere, in all things, and at all times.

There is an order to things and to the way the world emerges.
For Christians, God the Father eternally begets the Son (Word),
and the Spirit proceeds from the Father and the Word. Then the
world comes into existence. Finally, the human race emerges, a
creature capable of consciously reflecting on and participating in
God's creation. This Divine Order is important, as Christ-Followers
pray when they say, "Thy will be done on earth as it is in heaven"
(Matthew 6:10). There is peace and harmony when a proper order
is achieved, and it is the task of true spiritual leaders to seek this
order.

Our created existence is a small part of the vastness of God's orderly creation.
How does this insight impact how you order your thinking and acting?

CHAPTER 26

Movement begins at the place of rest,
    so a wise leader seeks the peaceful Center.
Silently seeking the Deep Light,
    wise shepherds are transformed by Deep Love

When active, a wise person is not easily impressed
    by outward appearances.
Looking deep beneath the surface,
    wise leaders calmly travel the path of Deep Light.

The wise shepherd recognizes the foolishness
    of striving for overt power over others.
It is better to nurture Deep Love,
    know yourself,
        and serve others.

A leader who embraces foolishness
    abandons Deep Light and loses touch with the Way.
A shepherd who becomes distracted by the world
    abandons Deep Love and forfeits true influence.

One who strays from the Way is forever off balance.

Remain Centered in Deep Light.
Act in Deep Love.

LISTEN TO ADVICE AND ACCEPT INSTRUCTION, THAT YOU MAY
GAIN WISDOM FOR THE FUTURE. THE HUMAN MIND MAY DEVISE
MANY PLANS, BUT IT IS THE PURPOSE OF THE LORD THAT WILL BE
ESTABLISHED.
(Proverbs 19:20–21 [NRSV])

Be Centered in the Word

Leadership is serious business. If a leader is hasty or unreflective, failure often results. This principle applies to families, businesses, churches, religious institutions, and governments—everywhere leadership is exercised.

It is important for leaders to make the best choice possible in complex and dangerous situations. Therefore, a wise person remains calm and thoughtful when evaluating a difficult decision and acts when the wisest course of action is finally revealed. When Jesus says, "I and the Father are one" (John 10:30), he is saying, among other things, "I have centered my being in the God of Israel. So, I think what the LORD thinks, and I do what the LORD does." Christ-Followers never perfectly achieve this identity of understanding and will with that of God, but should strive to achieve it.

Some people enjoy the active life; others enjoy a quiet life removed from the pressure of struggle and achievement. What kind of person are you? Can one be an active leader and still value contemplation? What does it mean to be both humble in waiting for insight into problems and active in seeking solutions?

CHAPTER 27

A skillful traveler leaves few marks on the path.
A skillful orator wastes few words in speaking.
A skillful business person instinctively calculates profit.
A skillful sailor ties knots that do not unravel.
A skillful dancer has instinctive grace on the dance floor.
A skillful, prudent person follows the Way through life.

A wise person seeks the best for everyone,
    rejecting no child of the One Who Is.
A wise person cherishes Creation,
    seeking the best for the lowliest creature.

This means embracing Deep Light.
This means suffering with Deep Love.

Therefore, the wise person reaches out to the foolish;
    the good reaches out to the wicked.
Rescuing the foolish and the broken,
    the wise shepherd embodies the Word.

Cherishing all things, wise shepherds
    follow the Great Shepherd.

        This is the dark, mysterious path of the Way.

SO FROM NOW ON WE REGARD NO ONE FROM A WORLDLY POINT OF
VIEW. THOUGH ONCE WE REGARDED CHRIST IN THIS WAY, WE DO
SO NO LONGER. THEREFORE, IF ANYONE IS IN CHRIST, HE IS A NEW
CREATION, THE OLD HAS GONE, THE NEW HAS COME! ALL THIS IS
FROM GOD, WHO RECONCILED US TO HIMSELF THROUGH CHRIST,
AND GAVE US THE MINISTRY OF RECONCILIATION . . .
(2 Corinthians 5:16–18 [NIV])

Nurture and Help Others Grow in Love

We live in a wasteful society. Materially, this results in "garbage
on the trail" of our lives. Mentally, we are surrounded by words,
from talk radio, to television, to music, to media and information
on the Internet. We have abundant possessions, perhaps too many.
Much of what we see, hear, and possess keeps us from seeing what
is really important. To be wise, we must remove the clutter from
our lives.

The wise person realizes that people are the most important
thing in life. Jesus is the one who "came to seek and to save what was
lost" (Luke 19:10). Saving people and assisting them in achieving
a wise life are the most important things Christ-Followers can do.
For Christ-Followers, reaching out to the suffering and lost in word
and deed is central to the wise life.

*Jesus tells the story of the prodigal son in order to suggest that
God never abandons anyone however far they have strayed (Luke 15:11–32).
Lao Tzu says that the wise rescue the foolish and wandering. How would your
priorities change if you took this seriously?*

CHAPTER 28

Know the principles of the active life;
    yet also embrace silence and stillness—
        the way of meditation and contemplation.

If you are able to become as a child
    in the face of adult problems,
        awaiting a revelation of the Word,
        you have found the Way.

One who embraces humble waiting on Deep Light
    knows the Way and is a pattern for the world.

One who waits for the Word in stillness
    never departs from the Way.
One who sincerely meditates before acting
    finds the path of Deep Light.

If in success you remain humbly centered on the Word,
    you are like a new plown field on a fertile farm.
You will bear much fruit.

If you remain simple while solving complex problems,
    you are like a child in the arms of the Word.
You will discern the best path in every situation.

The best deeds are done in simplicity and servanthood.

OUR SOUL WAITS FOR THE LORD; HE IS OUR HELP AND SHIELD.
OUR HEART IS GLAD IN HIM, BECAUSE WE TRUST IN HIS HOLY NAME.
LET YOUR STEADFAST LOVE, O LORD, BE UPON US EVEN AS WE
HOPE IN YOU.
(Psalm 33:20–22 [NRSV])

Waiting and Acting are both Virtues

The wise person knows success is a blessing, and mere activity does not guarantee accomplishment. Sometimes thoughtful waiting is the better path. The wise person also knows that waiting can become procrastination. There is a time to act. The wise life is a blend of stillness and action, contemplation and exertion, studying and putting to work what we have studied. It is important for wise living to understand and embody opposite traits of patience and activity. Jesus waited and prayed. He also cleansed the temple. In Christ, the virtues of meditation and virtuous activity were perfectly joined.

Athletes always attempt to keep their balance. Many mistakes result from being off balance. Part of the wisdom of any sport involves developing an intuitive sense of grace and balance. Moving too quickly or not moving at the right moment can cause many mistakes in athletics and daily life. The wise person combines quiet waiting and action, being and doing in a single personality. This virtue is hard to develop, and like any virtue, it takes practice.

How do you determine when to wait and when to act?
Does the metaphor of balance help you?

CHAPTER 29

A leader who desires to manage too many things
    certainly will be disappointed in the outcome.
The world is too fluid and complex to manage—
    it slips through grasping fingers like water.

The world is a spiritual reality and is harmed by violence.
Therefore, exercise prudent restraint.

Some people find leadership natural,
    others following.
Some people find striving natural;
    others accept life as it comes.
Some people are by nature strong,
    others weaker.
Some people find success in life;
    others meet with failure.

Accept people and things as they are.
Avoid extravagance, excess, and extremes.

      Abide in Deep Light.
      Embody Deep Love.
      Follow the Way.

AGAIN, THE DEVIL TOOK HIM TO A VERY HIGH MOUNTAIN AND
SHOWED HIM ALL THE KINGDOMS OF THE WORLD AND THEIR
SPLENDOR. "ALL THIS I WILL GIVE YOU," HE SAID, "IF YOU WILL
BOW DOWN AND WORSHIP ME." JESUS SAID TO HIM, "AWAY FROM
ME, SATAN! FOR IT IS WRITTEN, 'WORSHIP THE LORD YOUR GOD
AND SERVE HIM ONLY.'"
(Matthew 4:8–10 [NIV])

Avoid the Danger of Prideful Ambition

Some people are born to lead; others are born to follow.
Everyone is different and has a different place in the whole. The wise
person meditates on his or her limited capacities as well as on his or
her unlimited hopes, dreams, and desires. Such meditation allows
us to accept life as it comes. This is the secret of true fulfillment.

Uncontrolled ambition is the enemy of wisdom—especially in
leaders. Jesus asks, "What does it profit a person if he or she gains
the whole world, yet loses his or her own soul?" (Matthew 16:26).
Aggressive grasping and overreaching inevitably lead to disaster in
personal and public matters. We try to force solutions to intractable
problems. We have grandiose ideas and plans. They are too big for
our human limitations. The wise Christ-Follower respects human
limitations.

*What is your place in the whole and how can you learn to be happy in it? Why
is it important to avoid extravagance, excess, and extremes?*

CHAPTER 30

Those who wisely lead or assist those who lead
    avoid using force to attain an objective.
Wise shepherds resort to force or compulsion
    only when there is no other alternative.
Force normally brings a violent response;
    it is contrary to the Way.

A wise leader remembers this:
    the strong weaken over time.
Wherever there is conflict or coercion,
    true accomplishment seldom results.
Therefore, wise shepherds are patient.

Quietly and humbly achieve your objective.
A skillful leader attains an objective and then stops.
A shepherd with self-control does not overreach.
This is the path of the servant leader.

A wise shepherd never brags or boasts.
Such a leader serves others, not the False Self.
Centered in the Deep Light and filled with Deep Love,
    such a shepherd is truly and fully human.

Deep Love is violated by fighting and violence.
Conflict is not the deepest Way of the One Who Is.

I REALIZED ANOTHER THING, THAT IN THIS WORLD FAST RUNNERS DO NOT ALWAYS WIN THE RACES, AND THE BRAVE DO NOT ALWAYS WIN THE BATTLES. WISE MEN DO NOT ALWAYS EARN A LIVING, INTELLIGENT MEN DO NOT ALWAYS GET RICH, AND CAPABLE MEN DO NOT ALWAYS RISE TO HIGH POSITIONS. BAD LUCK HAPPENS TO EVERYONE.

(Ecclesiastes 9:11 [TEV])

Avoid Violence and Overreaching

Wise leaders remember the words of David, "You save the humble, but your eyes are on the haughty to bring them low" (2 Samuel 22:28). The way of pride and arrogance rarely brings lasting achievement. God always invisibly opposes pride and arrogance. God patiently opposes the violent and aggressive. The plans and the projects of the proud forever meet with inexplicable failure.

Force is a blunt instrument and is seldom as effective as cooperation. Forcing our way is almost never the wisest course of action in families, business, social organizations, churches, or government. Conflict normally breeds some future state of resentment and quarreling. Even where force is necessary, skillful leaders achieve an objective, and then stop. Humility and avoiding overreaching minimizes the negative aspects of conflict. Wise leaders never lose sight of the ultimate state of harmony they are seeking.

Physical violence is not the only kind of force that can be misused. What about words, or sex, or emotional manipulation? What kind of force do you sometimes use? Does force ultimately result in success?

CHAPTER 31

The best weapons are instruments of horror.
Those who follow the Way avoid their use.

Violence is contrary to Deep Light and Deep Love.
Conflict is not according to the Way.
Wise leaders value peace even in the midst of conflict.
Wise shepherds avoid violence and conflict—
　　resort to aggression only as a last resort.

Those who resort to aggression—
　　even from great necessity—
　　　　bring disorder into the world.

Conflict rarely brings the best result—
　　even the "victor" experiences the distortion
　　　　conflict brings upon the world.

Peace is the final objective of wise shepherds,
　　for conflict normally ends in confusion.
Lesser leaders rejoice in forced victory
　　and delight in carnage.

Wise leaders do not rejoice in conflict;
　　they understand the outcome will be disorder.
Disorder should be greeted with regret;
　　victory celebrations are occasions for grief.

TOO LONG HAVE I HAD MY DWELLING AMONG THOSE WHO HATE
PEACE. I AM FOR PEACE; BUT WHEN I SPEAK, THEY ARE FOR WAR.
(Psalms 120:7 [NRSV])

Value Peace and Harmony

David was a man of war, yet he knew peace was the ultimate
objective (Psalm 120:7). Jesus said, "Blessed are the peacemakers,
for they shall be called the sons of God" (Matthew 5:9). Even
the finest weapons are, in the end, instruments of destruction.
Even the most necessary conflict results in disorder of some kind.
Even the wisest leaders cannot foresee the consequences of conflict
for the organization or government they lead.

The wise person recognizes these facts and avoids the use
of force except where absolutely necessary and then only in a
proportionate and reasonable way. Every effort should be made to
maintain peace before a resort to conflict. Even in victory, the wise
person is humble, regarding the necessity of resort to arms as an
evil in and of itself. If we have been successful, it is only because of
the grace of the One Who Is.

*The Tao teaches that force should be used only as a last resort and then only as
part of the search for a livable peace. How might you put this into practice in
your home, business, family, and other relationships?*

CHAPTER 32

The eternal Word is beyond human words.
Although its Way appears contrary to human wisdom,
   those who follow it overcome the world.

Leaders who diligently follow the Way
   bless those who follow them.
Such shepherds serve the Kingdom of Heaven,
   bringing prosperity to the earth.

Thought begins with naming, and
   legislation begins with naming.
Yet, naming alone cannot create peace—
   for there is no end to reasoning.
People of the Way have little need for laws
   because Deep Love has created a new heart.

Only when the Word changes a heart
   is true peace found.

The Word is the Beginning and the End.
The Spirit is the river of the Word,
   creating life wherever it flows.

This is the source of a new heart.

I WILL PUT MY LAW IN THEIR MINDS AND WRITE IT ON THEIR HEARTS. I WILL BE THEIR GOD, AND THEY WILL BE MY PEOPLE. NO LONGER WILL A MAN TEACH HIS NEIGHBOR, OR A MAN HIS BROTHER, SAYING, "KNOW THE LORD," BECAUSE THEY WILL ALL KNOW ME, FROM THE LEAST OF THEM TO THE GREATEST . . . .
(Jeremiah 31:33–34 [NIV])

Lead from a Changed Heart

The Tao is "nameless," beyond conceptual definition by human words and phrases. Therefore, it cannot be conceptually known. The Word of God is rational and we can see it revealed in Christ, but we can never exhaust its depth of meaning.

Because Christ-Followers conceive of the Word as ultimately personal, it can only be known as a person is known, by personal, direct experience. Wisdom can never be achieved by abstract knowledge. Words are not enough. Only in prayerful simplicity, heart to heart, like little children, can Christians know the ways of God. This is why Jesus said, "Let the little children come to me and forbid them not, for such is the Kingdom of Heaven" (Matthew 19:14). There is no substitute for a new heart for those who follow the Way of Christ. Once we have received a new heart, the wise Christian discerns the best path forward with a practical childlike simplicity.

We live in world awash in laws. Do laws make people better? Often people do not obey laws once enacted. Why? What difference does it make to have a changed heart where obedience is concerned?

CHAPTER 33

Understand others and become wise.
Understand yourself and become wiser still.

Master others and become strong.
Master yourself and become stronger still.

Acquire money and material things and become wealthy.
Find contentment and become wealthier still.

Face adversity without flinching, and your will is strong.
Know when to compromise and endure hardship,
    and your heart becomes stronger still.

Those who follow the Way endure hardship.
Those who face death in the Word
    will not perish,
        but have life everlasting.

Those who lose their lives in service of Deep Love
    will find a life that does not end.

THEREFORE, I SAY TO YOU, DO NOT WORRY ABOUT YOUR LIFE,
WHAT YOU WILL EAT OR WHAT YOU WILL DRINK; NOR ABOUT YOUR
BODY, WHAT YOU WILL PUT ON. IS NOT LIFE MORE THAN FOOD AND
THE BODY MORE IMPORTANT THAN CLOTHING?
(Matthew 6:25 [NKJV])

Master Yourself and Endure Hardship

Superficially wise people understand others, master others, gain possessions, and seek success greater than others attain. The truly wise person gains self-understanding, masters himself or herself, is content with what life brings, and avoids unnecessary striving. Such a person is not forever concerned with mastering others and acquiring things. When trouble comes, they face it with calmness.

Self-mastery is one of the most important qualities of a leader. Self-possessed leaders live according to the Way and achieve true success and wisdom. This is especially true where there is conflict and adversity. Many failures of leadership come from a lack of self-mastery in conflict, not from a failure to understand people and situations. Self-discipline allows the wise person to delay gratification in the search for the common good. In this way many errors of judgment are avoided.

Do you feel you have a good understanding of yourself? When you think about yourself, what do you see as your strengths and weaknesses? Do you feel you can be your authentic self when interacting with others?

CHAPTER 34

The Word is the Ever-Present Deep Light
and Deep Love of the One Who Is.

Created things were created by and for the Word.
Existence and life depend upon the Word
sustaining everything by its invisible power.
Yet, the Word exercises authority humbly in Deep Love.
The Word embraces suffering and servanthood
toward the creation of the One Who Is.

The Spirit is also humble, claiming no glory for itself.
The Spirit points to the Word and the One Who Is,
creating and nourishing all things.
The Spirit embraces loving servanthood.
This is the power of Deep Love.

Wisdom does not seek greatness or acclaim;
it is humbly content to serve others—
and so accomplishes large tasks.

Deep Love serves others.
Deep Love transforms whomever it touches.

He is the image of the invisible God; his is the primacy over all creation. In him everything in heaven and on earth was created, not only things visible but also the invisible orders of thrones, sovereignties, and powers: the whole universe has been created through him and for him. He exists before all things, and all things are held together in him.

(Colossians 1:15–17 [REV])

Humble Service Holds Things Together

The *Tao Te Ching* considers the Tao to be everywhere, and everything depends on the unseen Tao. Christ-Followers understand Christ to be the Living Word of God who "was before all things, and in whom all things hold together" (Colossians 1:17). Christians do not visibly see the unseen Christ, but Christ-Followers do see the living and active spirit of Christ. The Spirit of Christ is everywhere. Yet, the Spirit is content to work in quiet, hidden love.

Like Christ, the wise person is content to work for good quietly in the background—a hard lesson in a society driven by celebrity. It is hard for leaders to learn this lesson. When leaders develop the ability to lead in humble service, they become true transformational leaders.

In what way does Jesus demonstrate the humility of God? Consider the natural human desire to succeed. What is the difference between immoderately seeking achievement and humbly using one's abilities and talents?

CHAPTER 35

Trust in the Word and lean upon its wisdom—
    journey through life without anxiety,
        a peace the world cannot give will come.

Hold fast to the Way amid storms of doubt—
    your heart's deepest need will be granted.
Embrace the voyage of Deep Love and Deep Light—
    the peace of Heaven's Kingdom will be yours.

Many linger where there is feasting;
    the silent wisdom of the Word attracts but a few.
The simplicity of Deep Love
    seems boring and unfashionable
        to those without the insight of Deep Light.
Seeing, there is nothing titillating to see.
Hearing, there is nothing to exciting hear.

One who receives the Word and walks the Way
    finds inexhaustible Deep Love and Deep Light

BE EVER HEARING, BUT NEVER UNDERSTANDING; BE SEEING, BUT
NEVER PERCEIVING. MAKE THE HEART OF THIS PEOPLE CALLOUSED,
MAKE THEIR EARS DULL AND CLOSE THEIR EYES. OTHERWISE
THEY MIGHT SEE WITH THEIR EYES, HEAR WITH THEIR EARS,
UNDERSTAND WITH THEIR HEARTS, AND TURN AND BE HEALED.
(Isaiah 6:9–10 [NIV])

Embrace the Priority of the Word

For those who are willing to embrace God and walk in the
way of Jesus, there is never ending joyful life. Jesus says, "I praise
you, Father, Lord of heaven and earth, because you have hidden
these things from the wise and learned, and revealed them to
little children" (Matthew 11:25). True wisdom (as opposed to
shrewdness) often seems insipid and tasteless. How can it possibly
be the inexhaustible source of life?

The Word is God's invisible, quiet presence. Yet, for many
people, this is not good enough. It does not smell of rich perfume.
It does not glitter like fine jewelry. It does not appear useful. Often,
wise living seems dull, weak, and colorless. Yet, in the end, it is the
source of joy and peace. Achieving a truly abundant life involves
recognizing a hidden wisdom concealed from the merely clever. It
involves a power that cannot be found by those who seek only to
dominate. It means seeking the Way of Christ.

*In what way is Jesus, the quiet Word of God, revealed to you? Do you listen for
the silent, hidden wisdom of the Word? How and when?*

CHAPTER 36

When the successful over-expand in pride,
    they inevitably contract and decline.
When the strong overexert because of their strength,
    they inevitably weaken and fade.
When those who oppose the good appear to succeed,
    they are near destruction.

If you want to possess the world,
    give everything away.
If you want victory over oppressors,
    serve them with compassion—
        give them your cloak before they ask.
If you want to live forever,
    bear your Cross and die to self.

Those who are flexible overcome the rigid.
Those who turn the other cheek overcome the strong.
Those who make peace inherit the earth.

As a great blue whale hides in deep waters
    and cannot be seen by anyone,
        a wise leader hides the source of his strength.

YOU HAVE HEARD THAT IT WAS SAID, "AN EYE FOR AN EYE, AND A TOOTH FOR A TOOTH." BUT I SAY TO YOU, DO NOT RESIST AN EVILDOER. BUT IF ANYONE STRIKES YOU ON THE RIGHT CHEEK, TURN THE OTHER ALSO; AND IF ANYONE WANTS TO SUE YOU AND TAKE YOUR COAT, GIVE YOUR CLOAK AS WELL.

(Matthew 5:38–40 [NRSV])

Humbly Serve the Highest Good

Often, among individuals, groups, and nations, there is a principle at work: People, groups, and nations achieve power, wealth, status, and great cultural achievements. Then, slowly but surely, they decay. The price of greatness is frequently slow dissolution. The price of riches is often weak materialism. Eventually, the weak overcome the strong, and the strong become weak.

The cause of this cycle is usually overreaching and pride. True wisdom and true strength are found in humility, self-control and service to others. Lasting achievements are not the great achievements of armies or political movements. Lasting achievements involve countless, often unheralded, people working for the good and a better future. Leaders who understand this principle, and who follow the Way, avoid pride and its consequences.

In the economy, times of over-expansion result in times of business contraction. Does it seem to also be a principle in other areas of life? Have you experienced this principle of expansion and contraction at work in your life? How and when?

CHAPTER 37

Meditate on the One Who Is.
Listen for the Word.
Wait on the Spirit.
Remember the value of the least action.
Abide in the Way.
Bring harmony to human relationships.
Maintain the peace of the One Who Is.

> Seek the Deep Light.
> Be open to its leading.
> Embrace Deep Love.
> Put to death the False Self
> Achieve simplicity.
> Act with discretion.

When leaders observe these principles—

> Meditate, Watch, Abide, and then Act

Then, the Word brings the future in peace.

This is the Way of the One Who Is.

THE LORD IS THE EVERLASTING GOD, THE CREATOR OF THE
ENDS OF THE EARTH. HE WILL NOT GROW TIRED OR WEARY, AND
HIS UNDERSTANDING NO ONE CAN FATHOM. HE GIVES STRENGTH
TO THE WEARY AND INCREASES THE POWER OF THE WEAK. EVEN
YOUTHS GROW TIRED AND WEARY, AND YOUNG MEN STUMBLE AND
FALL; BUT THOSE WHO HOPE IN THE LORD WILL RENEW THEIR
STRENGTH.
(Isaiah 40:28–31 [NIV])

Meditate and Wait Before Acting

In a culture characterized by frenetic activity, it is difficult to
recognize the virtue of inactivity. It helps to recognize that the
"inaction" recommended in the *Tao Te Ching* is not doing nothing at
all. The principle of inaction means doing nothing before the proper
time. It means doing only what is needed and avoiding unnecessary
action. It is a principle of conservation of energy. The principle of
inaction is a principle of timeliness. It is also a principle of acting
from a depth of simplicity and goodness.

The wise person does not wear himself or herself out with
unnecessary striving. This is why wisdom teaches, "Do not wear
yourself out to get rich; have the wisdom to show restraint"
(Proverbs 23:4). Acting wisely frees a person from the rush and
worries that so often complicate our lives. It allows the wise person
to wait and act with gentleness and tact.

Have you ever had to wait on God? What was the result?
How hard was it to just wait? What does it mean to act in simplicity
and peacefulness to bring about a result?

CHAPTER 38

A follower of the Way has a heart of virtue—
    an instinct of compassion and love.
A person of common virtue strives with human will;
    the virtue of love cannot be found by such a person.

A wise person abides in the Way
    and being genuine, accomplishes a good task.
A zealot forces virtue and is artificial;
    such a person accomplishes nothing.

When the Way is lost, only righteousness remains.
When righteousness is lost, only morality remains.
When morality is lost, only social custom remains.
When social custom is lost, there is chaos.
So, loss of the Way is the beginning of chaos.

The Way is a path of Deep Compassion.
A wise person seeks Deep Love and Deep Light.
This is the Way of Wisdom.

[B]E CLEAR MINDED AND SELF-CONTROLLED SO THAT YOU CAN
PRAY. ABOVE ALL, LOVE EACH OTHER DEEPLY, BECAUSE LOVE COVERS
OVER A MULTITUDE OF SINS. OFFER HOSPITALITY TO ONE ANOTHER
WITHOUT GRUMBLING. EACH ONE SHOULD USE WHATEVER GIFT
HE HAS RECEIVED TO SERVE OTHERS, FAITHFULLY ADMINISTERING
GOD'S GRACE IN ITS VARIOUS FORMS.
(I Peter 4:7–10 [NIV])

True Virtue Is Deep Compassion

The wise person is not always, or usually, consciously aware
of the nature of his or her virtue. It is a natural part of their
personality. This cannot be achieved all at once. There must be a
time of character formation when we are aware of our virtue (or
lack thereof). This kind of conscious virtue is commendable, but
there is a greater virtue to come. The greatest virtue is achieved
when it becomes a matter of habit. When virtue is a habit, we
unconsciously and reflexively do the correct thing.

Often, when the Way has been lost, people talk a great deal
about virtue, even write many books about virtue, but virtue itself
is missing. All that remains are rules of right and wrong and social
custom. We may live in just such a time. Recovering virtue involves
a slow process of transformation. There is no shortcut.

Losing our grounding in the Word has personal, family,
and social consequences. Have you ever lost your grounding in God?
What was the result in your life?

CHAPTER 39

The Word is Deep Love dwelling in Deep Light.

The heavens attain unity with the Word—there is light.
The earth attains unity with the Word—there is harmony.
Powers submit to the Word—there is order.
Fertile valleys submit to the Word—there is abundance.
Human beings submit to the Word—there is peace.
This is the influence of Deep Love and Deep Light.

Without the Word, the sky is dark.
Without the Word, the earth is unbalanced.
Without the Word, the powers are disordered.
Without the Word, fertile valleys are desolate.
Without the Word, human beings are violent.
Without the Word, leaders are prideful.

If leaders embrace humble service,
    those with power remember their roots.
Humility is, therefore, the greatest asset.

This is the Way of the Word.

WE KNOW HOW MUCH GOD LOVES US, AND WE HAVE PUT OUR
TRUST IN HIM. GOD IS LOVE, AND ALL WHO LIVE IN LOVE LIVE IN
GOD, AND GOD LIVES IN THEM.
(I John 4:16 [NLT])

The Best Leaders Embrace Deep Love

According to the *Tao Te Ching*, in ancient times, sages achieved
understanding of the Way and had clarity about the true nature of
things. Possessing this clarity, they were able to achieve compassion
and tranquility. Christ-Followers see the nature of virtue reflected
in the love of Christ. We achieve the virtue of this Deep Love by
becoming more like Christ. This is the true Way.

Those who achieve the virtue of Christ achieve the virtue of
the beatitudes: "Blessed are the meek, for they shall inherit the
earth" (Matthew 5:5). The meekness of which Jesus speaks is not
a lack of capacity but loving humility in the exercise of our natural
gifts. When we achieve this kind of gentleness, we instinctively
serve others and meet their deepest needs. If we fail to achieve this
kind of character, the result is some kind of disorder in human
relationships.

When you think of a humble leader, of whom do you think?
What characterizes a humble leader? In a world that often glorifies pride,
why does wisdom literature extol humility?

CHAPTER 40

The Word created all things from formless chaos.
The Spirit of the Word holds all things together.
All things return to the Word.
This is the Way of Heaven.

In stillness, the Spirit works.
In silence, the Spirit reveals.
In Light, the Spirit creates.
In Love, the Spirit sustains.

By Deep Light, the Word teaches.
By Deep Love, the Word redeems.

The Power of Deep Love,
    is the power of sacrificial self-giving.
This is the silent mystery of Deep Light—
    the power of Deep Love.

I SHALL SING ALWAYS OF THE LOVING DEEDS OF THE LORD;
THROUGHOUT ALL GENERATIONS I SHALL PROCLAIM YOUR
FAITHFULNESS. I SAID: YOUR LOVE WILL STAND FIRM FOREVER; IN
THE HEAVENS YOU HAVE ESTABLISHED YOUR FAITHFULNESS.
(Psalm 89:1–2 [REV])

The Mystery of Deep Light and Deep Love

The ancient Jews believed that by returning to God the people could be renewed. "Restore us to yourself, O LORD, that we may return; renew our days as of old, unless you have utterly rejected us and are angry with us beyond measure" (Lamentations 5:21–22). For the Taoist, the wise return to ancient wisdom of the Tao. It is in submission to the Tao that wisdom is found.

For Christ-Followers, by following the Way of Christ true wisdom is found. Christians believe that, in Christ, the fullness of God's love and wisdom are revealed. By this Word, the world was created. Faith in Christ is the way to experience and possess this deep wisdom and love. Faith, and the Love and Hope which faith brings, is also the source of true virtue and of eternal life. Because of their experience of this Faith, Hope and Love, the wise person is never afraid to suffer for others or creation.

*Do you agree that God works most powerfully in invisible silence?
How does the Word work in your life? In what ways do you practice
listening for the silent voice of Deep Love and Deep Light?*

CHAPTER 41

When excellent people hear the Word,
    they diligently follow the Way.
When double-minded people hear the Word,
    they believe and follow halfheartedly.
When worldly people hear the Word,
    they ridicule the whole idea.

To the foolish and overly aggressive:

> The wisdom of the Word seems foolish.
> The power of Deep Love seems weak.
> The Way appears to lead nowhere.
> Wholesomeness seems deficient.
> Virtue seems inadequate.

The Word is not heard with human ears.
Deep Light is not seen with human eyes.
Deep Love is beyond the human heart.

The Word abides in the eternal One Who Is,
    yet the Word nourishes
        and brings to completion all things.

A FARMER PLANTED SEED. AS HE SCATTERED THE SEED, SOME FELL
ON THE ROAD, AND BIRDS ATE IT. SOME FELL IN THE GRAVEL; IT
SPROUTED QUICKLY BUT DIDN'T PUT DOWN ROOTS, SO WHEN THE
SUN CAME UP IT WITHERED JUST AS QUICKLY. SOME FELL IN THE
WEEDS; AS IT CAME UP, IT WAS STRANGLED BY THE WEEDS. SOME
FELL ON GOOD EARTH, AND PRODUCED A HARVEST BEYOND HIS
WILDEST DREAMS.
(Matthew 13:3–8 [Message])

Wise People See What Others Miss

Jesus told the "Parable of the "Four Soils" (See, Matthew
13:10–23; Mark 4:1–13; Luke 8:4–8) to illustrate the response of
people to the Word. When sown, some seed falls on a rocky path
and never germinates. Some seed falls where there is little topsoil.
It germinates but dies when the heat of trouble comes. Some seed
falls among thorn bushes. It is choked by cares and worries. Some
seed falls on good ground and bears a crop.

The *Tao Te Ching* speaks of different types of people who hear its
wisdom. The best people hear and practice the Way. Next are those
who hear but only half believe. Finally, there are those who laugh at
wisdom. They cannot recognize the path that leads to fulfillment.
Each person must decide what kind of soil he or she will be. Will
we abide in the Word and bear fruit in the way of Wisdom? Or.
Will we live on the shallow, rocky path of foolishness?

Some people seek wisdom with all of their hearts, some half-heartedly,
some not at all. What kind of person are you?

CHAPTER 42

The Triune One always was and always is.
The Word is begotten of the Father of all things.
The Spirit proceeds from the Father and the Word.
The Triune One is bound together in Deep Love.

All things reflect the Deep Light of the Word;
    all things exist by the Deep Love of the Word.
In true relationship, there is perfect harmony.
In harmony is the peace of the One Who Is.

No one wants to be orphaned, widowed, or poor.
Yet, those who follow the Way
    embrace the circumstances of life
        dwelling in the Deep Love
           of the One Who Is and Will Be.

Those who lose their life will gain life.
Those who gain their life will lose life.

This is what the Word teaches:

> "Those who live by the sword
> die by the sword."

IF ANYONE WOULD COME AFTER ME, HE MUST DENY HIMSELF AND
TAKE UP HIS CROSS DAILY AND FOLLOW ME. FOR WHOEVER WANTS
TO SAVE HIS LIFE WILL LOSE IT, BUT WHOEVER LOSES HIS LIFE FOR
ME WILL SAVE IT. WHAT GOOD IS IT FOR A MAN TO GAIN THE
WHOLE WORLD, AND YET LOSE OR FORFEIT HIS VERY SELF?
(Luke 9:23–25 [NIV])

Self-Denial Is a Powerful Thing

For Taoists, harmony is achieved by following the Tao. For
Christians, the Way of Christ is the path that leads to peace with
God, healthy relations with other people, and harmony with
nature. This is achieved through the kind of wisdom that practices
simplicity, self-denial, and humble service. For those caught up in
the world, this seems like a loss of power, possessions, and success.
For those who see the true nature of the universe, it is the very
wisdom of God.

There is a price to be paid to follow the Way. The *Bible* says,
"If anyone would come after me, he must take up his Cross and
follow me" (Luke 9:26). The price of true wisdom is self-denial.
Dying to our natural self and our natural desires is a price we are
never naturally willing to pay. It requires the supernatural work of
the Spirit of Christ.

*Jesus says, "Those who find their life will lose it, and those who lose their life for
my sake will find it" (Matthew 10:39 [NRSV]). How does this work? What
part of your life do you need to lose to achieve wholeness?*

CHAPTER 43

Those who accept Reality adapt and conform to it.
Those who adapt to Reality overcome difficulties.
Like a slowly moving stream,
    which offers little resistance,
        yet eventually carves a great and deep valley,
            the Way prevails over difficulties.

Truly wise people listen to the silent Word.
Truly wise people perceive the Deep Light.
Truly wise people comprehend
    the quiet teaching of the One Who Is.

Only those who embrace Deep Love
    understand the value of active acceptance
        and peaceful resistance.

This is how followers of the Way
    understand the silent illumination of Deep Light
        and the quiet power of Deep Love.

BE PATIENT, THEREFORE, BELOVED, UNTIL THE COMING OF THE
LORD. THE FARMER WAITS FOR THE PRECIOUS CROP FROM THE
EARTH, BEING PATIENT WITH IT UNTIL IT RECEIVES THE EARLY AND
THE LATE RAINS. YOU ALSO MUST BE PATIENT.
(James 5:7–8 [NRSV])

Remember the Power of Persistence

In difficult circumstances, it is easy to become impatient and lash out against others. Wisdom teaches: "Better is a patient person than a warrior, one who controls his temper is greater than one who takes a city" (Proverbs 16:32). Violence and aggression only appear to be the way to success. In truth, history shows that the weak often overcome the strong. Aggressive people often wear themselves out in ceaseless conflict.

The wise person allows events to take their course. The wise leader creates the least possible disruption by avoiding conflict. Persistence is the ability to act patiently over a long period of time in the face of temptation to the contrary, including the temptation to aggressive behavior. Love is like the waters of a river that slowly, slowly, over time, carves a deep valley. Eventually, love will have its victory.

Do you believe that there is value in passively resisting evil?
What would it involve for you to learn to be like water: patiently,
constantly and peacefully working on problems?

CHAPTER 44

Which is more important?
    A good name or endless years of life?
Which is more valuable?
    Belongings or a simple, virtuous life?
Which is more destructive?
    Achievement or disappointment?

Knowing when and how to die to self and selfish desire
    is the secret of true virtue.
Knowing when you have enough
    is the secret to wholeness and peace.
Knowing how to accept failure
    is the secret of true accomplishment.

Knowing when to stop avoids over-extension.
Deep Love seeks harmony over achievement.
This is the secret of enduring success.

Followers of the Way understand
    the power of Sacrificial Love,
        the power of Cruciform Love.

This is the way to abundant, eternal life

A GOOD NAME IS TO BE CHOSEN RATHER THAN GREAT RICHES, AND
FAVOR IS BETTER THAN SILVER OR GOLD.
(Proverbs 22:1 [NRSV])

Preserve Your Good Name

What is most important in life? Wealth? Power? Possessions?
The wise person recognizes that a good name, a healthy family, a
job well done, and a community well served are more important
than wealth or success. Jesus told a parable about a man with many
barns. He spent his entire life acquiring things, waiting for the day
when he could retire. But God said to the man, "You fool! This
very night your life will be demanded from you. Then who will get
what you have prepared for yourself?" (Luke 12:20).

Knowing when to stop striving is a most important aspect
of wise living. Putting an end to ceaseless striving allows us to
concentrate on what is really important in life: a reputation created
by loving service to God and others. The most important virtue we
can possess in achieving a balanced life is the discipline that comes
from self-giving love. Knowing when to stop serving ourselves and
start serving others is the first and most important step toward
balanced living.

*How would your life change if you committed to value loving God and others
more than anything else? What would people then associate with your name?*

CHAPTER 45

The brokenness of the world cannot be fully healed.
Excellent accomplishments remain partial and flawed.
Completion of a noble task is soon forgotten.
It is enough to achieve the possible
    while diligently following the Way.
Do not wear yourself out attempting the impossible.

The straightest line often seems crooked.
The adept performer often seems clumsy.
The greatest speaker often seems to stammer.
The highest people often seem lowly.
Look, then, beneath the surface.

As movement overcomes cold,
    and stillness overcomes heat,
        quietly embodying the Word brings peace.

This is the humble service of the Way.

I URGE, THEN, FIRST OF ALL, THAT REQUESTS, PRAYERS,
INTERCESSION AND THANKSGIVING BE MADE FOR EVERYONE— FOR
KINGS AND ALL THOSE IN AUTHORITY, THAT WE MAY LIVE PEACEFUL
AND QUIET LIVES IN ALL GODLINESS AND HOLINESS. THIS IS GOOD,
AND PLEASES GOD OUR SAVIOR, WHO WANTS ALL MEN TO BE SAVED
AND TO COME TO KNOWLEDGE OF THE TRUTH.
(I Timothy 2:1–4 [NIV])

Value Imperfect Accomplishments

The perfectionist tries to solve problems once and for all. This
is a mistake. All accomplishments are incomplete. All victories are
temporary. No accomplishment is without its weaknesses. Every
victory leaves another enemy ready to emerge. Every honor will
someday be forgotten. This is the nature of life.

Looking beyond appearances, a wise person follows the
Way, understanding the important, but relative value of worldly
accomplishment. Such a person sees that what appears to be
a difficult and winding path may be the best way to achieve an
objective. Such a person recognizes that improving a situation is
sufficient if improvement is all that can be achieved. This allows
a wise person to live a life of quiet virtue, trusting in God for
the future. It allows a wise leader to avoid perfectionism and
overreaching.

*One of the most encouraging teachings of the Tao is that our accomplishments can
be imperfect and yet valuable. In your life, what would it mean to give up seeking
perfection and concentrate on the possible?*

CHAPTER 46

When humankind follows the Way,
    there is peace and prosperity.
When humankind does not follow the Way,
    there is conflict and famine.

There is no misfortune greater than selfish craving.
There is no calamity greater than pervasive discontent.
There is no catastrophe greater than unrestrained greed.
There is no disaster greater than conflict.

Where there is contentment with enough,
    the One Who Is gives the blessing of peace.

WHAT STARTS WARS AND FIGHTS AMONG YOU? ISN'T IT THE
WHOLE ARMY OF EVIL DESIRES AT WAR WITHIN YOU? YOU WANT
WHAT YOU DON'T HAVE, SO YOU SCHEME AND KILL TO GET IT . . .
AND THE REASON YOU DON'T HAVE WHAT YOU WANT IS THAT YOU
DON'T ASK GOD FOR IT. AND EVEN WHEN YOU DO ASK, YOU DON'T
GET IT BECAUSE YOUR WHOLE MOTIVE IS WRONG— YOU WANT
ONLY WHAT WILL GIVE YOU PLEASURE.
(James 4:1–4 [NLT])

Avoid the Conflict Greed Creates

The *Tao Te Ching* teaches that conflict is a symptom the Way is
being ignored. In the book of James, the author identifies *immoderate
desire* as the root cause of conflict. First Timothy teaches, ". . . the
love of money is a root of all kinds of evil. Some people, eager for
money, have wandered from the faith and pierced themselves with
many griefs" (1 Timothy 6:10). Not satisfied with what we have,
we seek more. Greed is one of the greatest moral calamities that
humans can experience, and excessive striving for money leads to
much suffering.

When the Way is followed, peace rules because desires are
controlled. When the Way is ignored human pride, human desire,
and human greed are unrestrained. The result is conflict. And,
violent conflict is always a calamity.

*Do you think of selfishness, discontent, and greed as great misfortunes?
Are they? Why or why not? Is greed a part of your life? If greed is a part of
your life, in what way can you eliminate it?*

CHAPTER 47

Anyone, however simple, can know and follow the Way.

A person can follow the Way
    without leaving his or her neighborhood.
A person can see the Deep Light
    without traveling to a far country.
A person can be filled with Deep Love
    in a windowless room—a prayer closet.

Sometimes, the more a person seeks knowledge,
    the less is understood;
Sometimes, the less one seeks knowledge,
    the more is understood.

Wise people understand without departing.
Wise people see without looking abroad.
Wise people accomplish things without frenetic activity.

The Wise:

> Seek the One Who Is
> Center in the Word
> Act in the Spirit.

HERE IS A LAST PIECE OF ADVICE. IF YOU BELIEVE IN GOODNESS
AND IF YOU VALUE THE APPROVAL OF GOD, FIX YOUR MINDS ON
WHATEVER IS TRUE AND HONORABLE AND JUST AND PURE AND
LOVELY AND PRAISEWORTHY.
(Philippians 4:8–9 [Phillips])

Acquire the Grace of Simple Wisdom

The rise of modern science brought an interest in the world
and in investigating physical reality. For the past three hundred
years, the peoples of Western Europe have roamed restlessly around
the world, spreading a civilization that is intensely materialistic,
scientific, and technological. This time of ceaseless striving has
produced plenty for many people, but it has not produced goodness
or peace.

The most important moral and spiritual lessons do not require
ceaseless activity. They are learned as we contemplate the ways of
God. We cannot learn these lessons until we quietly listen. Like
the Psalmist, we must say, "I do not concern myself with great
matters or things too wonderful for me. I have stilled and quieted
my soul like child with its mother…." (Psalm 131:1–2). When we
are willing to cut off the pressure of activities and possessions and
listen for the voice of the Spirit, we have taken the first step towards
wise and wholesome living.

The Way of Wisdom is simple, but very few people actually follow it. Jesus
teaches, "[M]y yoke is easy and my burden is light" (Matthew 11:30 [NIV]),
but few people take it on. What does this tell us about others and ourselves?

CHAPTER 48

People who seek worldly wisdom and knowledge
    try to learn something new every day.
People who seek the Way
    try to unlearn false wisdom every day.
When false wisdom vanishes like the night,
    the humility of the Word is achieved.

When followers of the Way
    are filled with Uncreated Light and Love,
        all that must be done is gracefully accomplished;
            nothing important remains undone.

Those who trust in the Word
    overcome the world without striving.
Those who frantically attempt good deeds
    accomplish little of lasting value.

If you would change the world:

        Change yourself.
        Be still before the Word.
        Do not force events.
        Allow tranquility to come.
        Follow the Way.

FOR WHERE THERE IS ENVY AND SELFISH AMBITION, THERE WILL
ALSO BE DISORDER AND WICKEDNESS OF EVERY KIND. BUT THE
WISDOM FROM ABOVE IS FIRST PURE; THEN PEACEABLE, GENTLE,
WILLING TO YIELD, FULL OF MERCY AND GOOD FRUITS, WITHOUT
A TRACE OF PARTIALITY OR HYPOCRISY. AND A HARVEST OF
RIGHTEOUSNESS IS SOWN IN PEACE.
(James 3:16–18 [NRSV])

Unlearn False Wisdom; Learn True Wisdom

There is a kind of active intelligence that tests and adopts every
new and innovative idea. This strategy works well in the fields of
science and technology, but not in matters of faith and morals.
In these areas, ceaseless innovation often leads to confusion and
faddism.

Those who follow the Way must unlearn a false and worldly
shrewdness and learn again the simplest truths of the human soul.
The secret of this wisdom is respect for those who lived before
us and faced many of the same temptations and difficulties. Such
people have a deep appreciation for the wisdom of those who lived
in prior ages and faced the basic problems of life wisely and well.
This is the way spiritual and moral wisdom is found. When such
wisdom is discovered, we are content to wait, to pray, and to act
only at the proper time.

What things do you need to remember to become wise?
What things do you need to forget in order to achieve wisdom and happiness?
What things are you doing that you need to stop doing? What things are you not
doing that you need to start doing?

CHAPTER 49

If you want to understand the world:

> Remain open to Reality.
> Seek the Deep Light.
> Humbly listen to the Word.
> Achieve Deep Love for People and Creation.
> Act according to the Way.

Followers of the Way
     treat friends and good people
          as persons of value and worth.
With wise restraint and caution,
     they treat enemies and worthless people
          with the same grace.

Those who follow the Way
     are honest to those who are honest.
Those who follow the Way
     are also honest to those who are dishonest.

If you do this, everyone will trust you.

Wise shepherds act without prejudice.
Wise leaders await a true perception of reality.
Seeking the good of all,
     such leaders follow the Good Shepherd.

IT IS THE GLORY OF GOD TO CONCEAL A MATTER; TO SEARCH OUT
A MATTER IS THE GLORY OF KINGS. AS THE HEAVENS ARE HIGH AND
THE EARTH IS DEEP, SO THE HEARTS OF KINGS ARE UNSEARCHABLE.
REMOVE THE DROSS FROM THE SILVER, AND OUT COMES MATERIAL
FOR THE SILVERSMITH; REMOVE THE WICKED FROM THE KING'S
PRESENCE, AND HIS THRONE WILL BE ESTABLISHED THROUGH
RIGHTEOUSNESS.
(Proverbs 25:1–5 [NIV])

Conform Action to Reality

Prejudice is the enemy of wisdom. So, the wise person avoids "fixed ideas," by which the *Tao Te Ching* means ideas contrary to changing reality. A well-trained mind maintains flexibility in adapting to reality. Flexibility of mind always involves sensitivity in understanding and working with others.

The wise person treats all persons fairly and promotes honesty and goodness. As Jesus put it, "Do unto others as you would have others do unto you" (Matthew 7:12). This requires a constant evaluation of what the law of love requires in each situation. The wise person searches out the truth of a situation, and then acts in love. In particular, when we see every human being as a child of God, we learn to treat everyone as a child of God. When we put the law of love into practice, we end up treating everyone with loving grace.

What does it mean to remain flexible and open to reality in making decisions?
What does it mean to treat all people with sensitivity and grace?

CHAPTER 50

All people enter the world at the moment of birth
and leave at the moment of death:

A few follow the Path of Life,
others follow the Path of Destruction,
many simply pass through Life to Death.
Only a very few are wise.
What is the reason for this?

Most people are afraid of dying to their False Self,
and so, do not find eternal life before death.

Those who follow the Way
face danger with courage and Deep Love.

When facing danger and conflict,
they act wisely, embodying Deep Light.

When attacked, weapons cannot harm them.
Followers of the Way are beyond the power of death.
Even if they die, death cannot hold them.
This is the power of Deep Love.

OH, THE JOYS OF THOSE WHO DO NOT FOLLOW THE ADVICE OF
THE WICKED, OR STAND AROUND WITH SINNERS, OR JOIN IN WITH
SCOFFERS. BUT THEY DELIGHT IN DOING EVERYTHING THE LORD
WANTS; DAY AND NIGHT THEY THINK ABOUT HIS LAW. THEY ARE
LIKE TREES PLANTED ALONG THE RIVERBANK BEARING FRUIT EACH
SEASON WITHOUT FAIL. THEIR LEAVES NEVER WITHER; AND IN ALL
THEY DO THEY PROSPER.
(Psalm 1:1–3 [NLT]).

Die to Selfish Desire

Very few people seek wisdom and the Way in daily life. Most
people follow whatever custom is prevalent in their society or social
group. Others either engage in self-destructive behavior or fill their
lives with ceaseless activities, just trying to get by.

Those who follow the Way appreciate the wisdom God wove
into the fabric of the universe. This wisdom has been revealed to
wise men and prophets, and then was fully revealed to us in Jesus
Christ. People with this kind of wisdom do not try to escape
responsibilities. They accept suffering as part of life. They die to
selfish desire. They are calm in the face of difficulties. Such people
are free of selfish ambition. They are not motivated by false pride.
They are not afraid of the future. They have moved from natural
to supernatural living.

*Can you think of a time when you died to yourself and found that in so doing
you achieved a greater happiness? Why is dying to self important in seeking
abundant life?*

Chapter 51

The One Who Is begets the Word.
The Word orders creation by Uncreated Deep Light.
The Spirit creates and sustains all things
    through ever present Uncreated Deep Love.

The Word creates silently, like a whisper,
    without force freely nurturing everything
        by Deep Love and Deep Light.

The Word gives order, reason, and harmony;
    its Deep Light permeates creation.
The Word gives freedom and nurture;
    its Deep Love sustains and protects all things.
All things were made by the Word,
    yet the silent Word remains a servant.

Beneath the flux and change of the created order,
    Deep Light and Deep Love work in silence,
        the silence of the eternal Word.

This is the great mystery of the ages.

THE LORD FORMED ME FROM THE BEGINNING, BEFORE HE CREATED
ANYTHING ELSE. I WAS APPOINTED IN AGES PAST, AT THE VERY
FIRST, BEFORE THE EARTH BEGAN . . . I WAS THERE WHEN HE
ESTABLISHED THE HEAVENS, WHEN HE DREW THE HORIZON ON THE
OCEANS . . . I WAS THERE WHEN HE SET THE LIMITS OF THE SEAS,
SO THEY WOULD NOT SPREAD BEYOND THEIR BOUNDARIES. AND
WHEN HE MARKED OFF THE EARTH'S FOUNDATIONS, I WAS THE
ARCHITECT AT HIS SIDE.
(Proverbs 8:22–23, 27, 29–30 [NLT])

Be Created and Recreated by Deep Light

Taoists believe the Tao produces all things. It is the source of all
that is. The Tao cultivates and nurtures all things. Christ-Followers
believe the Word of God (Logos) is the personal Reality through
which God, in Divine Love, created and nurtures all things. Through
his Divine Light God gives wisdom and eternal life. By indwelling
the Way of Jesus, we are changed by faith into new people.

When we live in constant fellowship with God and treat people
and things according to the Word, there is peace, what the Jews
referred to as "Shalom." We are created and recreated in the image
of the One who was God's shalom incarnate. Then, and only then,
do we find wholeness and peace. We achieve this peace as we receive
the life, nurture, protection, and growth that only God can give. In
the end, we receive eternal life as we return to the One in Whom all
things find life and completion.

In what way do you want to be recreated and renewed in the image of Christ?
Are you ready to receive it as a gift?

CHAPTER 52

There was a beginning
    when the One Who Is created all things.
All things were created and are yet being created
    by the Word and its Deep Light
        as Deep Love seeks Deep Peace.

Children of the Word are children of Deep Love.
Children of the Word are children of Deep Light.
The Path of Wisdom is the path
    of Deep Love and Deep Light.
This is the Way.

Wisdom is the lovely mother of virtue.
Virtue is the beautiful mother of discretion.

Love silence.
Embrace simplicity.
You will be without cares.

Love to chatter.
Have lavish taste.
You will always be anxious.

Pay attention to details.
Know when to cease.
Seek a true vision of Reality.

HAPPY ARE THOSE WHO FIND WISDOM, AND THOSE WHO GET UNDERSTANDING, FOR HER INCOME IS BETTER THAN SILVER, AND HER REVENUE BETTER THAN GOLD. SHE IS MORE PRECIOUS THAN JEWELS, AND NOTHING YOU DESIRE CAN COMPARE WITH HER.
(Proverbs 3:13–15 [NRSV]).

Love Silence, Embrace Simplicity, Seek the True Way

Christianity and Taoism believe there is an ultimate reality— the Triune God, Father, Son and Holy Spirit in Christianity and the Tao in Taoism. This ultimate reality is the womb and beginning of all things. Wisdom is achieved by living in conformity with this reality. As a first step to wise living, a person must recognize that there is an ultimate reality. Then, a person must ask the question, "What is the character of ultimate reality to which my thinking and acting must conform to live wisely and well?"

For Christ-Followers, the ultimate reality is the God of Eternal Light and Eternal Love. The person who finds this wisdom has found the most precious thing of all (Proverbs 3:13-15). Those who embrace silence, center themselves, avoid meddling in the affairs of others, and live simply. Such people wisely live in harmony with the ultimate reality of the God who is Love and Light. This divine love guides and sustains the believer throughout all of life and into eternity.

What does it mean to love simplicity? How would your life be different if you were to seek simplicity? Can you think of a way in which your life is overly-complicated?

CHAPTER 53

The Way is the Path of Life:
Understand one thing—the Word.
Follow one path wherever it leads—the Way.

Fear above all things straying from the Way;
straying from the Way results in trouble.

Here is how to stray from the Way
and begin to be in want:

Spend lavishly
Neglect business
Seek pleasure.

Wearing expensive clothes and jewelry,
filling ourselves with expensive food and drink,
wasting money on useless possessions,
squandering time on entertainment—
this is excessive
and contrary to the Way.

BE SURE YOU KNOW THE CONDITION OF YOUR FLOCKS, GIVE
CAREFUL ATTENTION TO YOUR HERDS; FOR RICHES DO NOT ENDURE
FOREVER, AND A CROWN IS NOT SECURE FOR ALL GENERATIONS.
(Proverbs 27:23–24 [NIV])

Avoid Luxury, Work Diligently

Jesus says, "Enter through the narrow gate. For wide is the
gate and broad is the way that leads to destruction, and many enter
through it. But small is the gate and narrow the way that leads to
life, and only a few find it" (Matthew 7:13–14). Foolishness is a
broad, easy path; wisdom is a narrow path and difficult to follow.
A life motivated by desire and directed by conformity to fads and
changing fashion is ultimately foolish. A life led by the ethos of a
consumer-driven culture is ultimately unwise.

The wise life involves restraint of desire, avoidance of mere
luxury, hard work, and attention to detail. This way is not easy,
and it is especially not easy for leaders, who are constantly exposed
to the temptation to acquire more goods and more luxury. The
antidote to the pressure of desire is to reject our society's constant
emphasis on pleasure-seeking, cultivate simplicity, and pay single-
minded attention to the business at hand. Such persons find a
kind of wholeness denied those who embrace the faddishness and
materialism of our culture.

Wisdom teaches that, when we begin to require and seek extravagant things and
an extravagant lifestyle, we often end up poorer as a result. Why is this true?
Can you think of a way this has been true in your life?

CHAPTER 54

One who builds upon the Word
    will not be washed away by trouble.
Embrace wisdom and you will find true security
    for yourself, your family,
        and your children's children.

If the Way is carefully cultivated in a person;
    virtue grows and becomes genuine.
If the Way is carefully cultivated in a family,
    virtue will grow by loving transmission.
If the Way is carefully cultivated in a community,
    virtue will grow through careful schooling.
If the Way is carefully cultivated in a nation,
    virtue will grow by wise leadership.
If the Way is carefully cultivated in the world,
    virtue will grow as the Way is followed.

Evaluate a person by what a person is.
Evaluate a family by what a family is.
Evaluate a community by what a community is.
Evaluate a country by what a country is.
Evaluate the world by what the world is.

How will you know this is true?
Observe and see.

EVERYONE THEN WHO HEARS THESE WORDS OF MINE AND ACTS
ON THEM IS LIKE A WISE MAN WHO BUILT HIS HOUSE ON THE ROCK.
THE RAIN FELL, THE FLOODS CAME, AND THE WINDS BLEW AND
BEAT ON THAT HOUSE; BUT IT DID NOT FALL, BECAUSE IT HAD BEEN
FOUNDED ON THE ROCK.
(Matthew 7:24–25 [NRSV])

Build Your Life on the Way

Virtue begins with individual character development. It is
cultivated in family life. From the family, virtue spreads to the local
community. Finally, virtue comes to a nation. In the modern world,
we attempt to form character using programs in schools and other
institutions. These are attempts are not sufficient. Such attempts
ignore the organic way in which wisdom is acquired and character
formed. They are doomed to ultimate failure.

People and societies must build lives founded on virtue. The
only way to achieve virtue is the slow path of personal change,
family change, community change, and so on. The wise person
does not ignore what can be done to promote virtue by the wise
functioning of public institutions. Yet, the wise person understands
that public institutions, cannot replace personal commitment and
family involvement. There is no shortcut to good character.

*How do you judge people and situations? If you were to
apply this teaching to yourself, your family, your community,
your nation, what would your judgment be?*

CHAPTER 55

One born of the Spirit
    by the birth pangs of Deep Love
        has the power of New Life, like a child
            clinging to its mother's breast.

Have the life of a newborn child!
Grow in the grace of the One Who Is.
Experience the protection of the Word.

To achieve the peace and protection of the Way,
    live simply according to the Word.
To know the Way throughout life,
    be filled with the wisdom of Deep Light.

To extend life unnaturally is unwise.
Death comes to everyone sooner or later.

When the Will to Power is unrestrained,
    the Word is absent and chaos results.

When the flower reaches full bloom, it decays.
When people reach their prime, they begin to age.
Although the Word is eternal, creation is not.
Decay is the way of created things.
Action contrary to the Way hastens decay.

I TELL YOU THE TRUTH, NO-ONE CAN ENTER THE KINGDOM OF
GOD WITHOUT BEING BORN OF WATER AND THE SPIRIT. FLESH
GIVES BIRTH TO FLESH, BUT THE SPIRIT GIVES BIRTH TO SPIRIT.
(John 3:5–6 [NIV])

Be Filled with New Life

"To know harmony means to be in accord with the eternal,"
says the *Tao Te Ching*. Those who live contrary to the Way complicate
and shorten their lives. The wise person lives in accord with the
physical and moral order of the universe. When we humbly accept
this order, we develop a childlike simplicity, an openness and
teachability born of love and respect for God. We are nurtured in
wisdom and strengthened to face the challenges of life.

Jesus said, "Let the little children come to me, and do not
hinder them, for the kingdom of heaven belongs to such as these"
(Matthew 19:14). The first step to wise living involves developing a
childlike, faithful dependence on the One Who Is. When we do, we
receive the gift of God's Spirit, a spirit of new, eternal life. We find
harmony with God, with creation, and with other people. Then,
gradually we are filled with wisdom for living. Such people know
what it is like to experience Eternal Life, now, in this world. They
are not afraid to let go of things which will pass away. They have
found the Kingdom of Heaven.

There is a cycle to life, from birth, to maturity, to decay to death.
Should we resist this cycle or accept it? When we receive the gift of a new
spiritual life, what happens to this cycle?

CHAPTER 56

Those who understand wisdom refrain from talking.
Those who chatter on and on show their ignorance.
Remember: the One Who Is speaks in silence.

Learn the virtue of silence.
Quietly ponder every situation.
Contemplate the world with humility.
Let go of prejudice, presumption, and arrogance.
Allow your heart to be filled with wisdom.

> Achieve Inner Quiet.
> Find the Center.
> Become one with Reality.
> Seek the One Who Is.
> Abide in the Word.

Such persons are not easily upset
    by the whims and acts of others.
Such persons are not easily deceived
    by the strategies and manipulations of others.
Indifferent to honor and dishonor,
    they follow the Way wherever it leads.

HE WHO RESTRAINS HIS WORDS HAS KNOWLEDGE, AND HE WHO
HAS A COOL SPIRIT IS A MAN OF UNDERSTANDING. EVEN A FOOL
WHO KEEPS SILENT IS CONSIDERED WISE; WHEN HE CLOSES HIS LIPS,
HE IS DEEMED INTELLIGENT.
(Proverbs 17:27–28 [RSV])

Value Wise Silence; Trust the Way

Jesus said, "I am the vine; you are the branches. If a man remains in me and I in him, he will bear much fruit; apart from me you can do nothing" (John 15:5). In the end, faith merges into a mystic experience of oneness with God. There is a story told of St. Thomas Aquinas, the great medieval theologian. He spent his life trying to understand God. Near the end of his life, he had a mystic encounter with God. The result was a profound sense that all the words he had written were nothing compared to the Divine Reality. God simply defies our attempts at complete understanding.

Silence is the most profound teacher. In silence, the most profound lessons are learned. In silence, we become open to God's eternal, quiet voice. When we silently ponder the complexity of life, we learn to simplify problems. When we quietly enter God's living presence, we are finally able to quietly commune with God's Word. In that silence, we find the Center from which wisdom comes.

*All wisdom literature speaks of the importance of the tongue
and the virtue of silence. In what ways do you need to learn about
the importance of silence and speaking carefully? How can silence make
us better able to wisely use our tongues?*

CHAPTER 57

The best shepherds have deep sacrificial integrity;
    such leaders emulate the Incarnate Word.
Authority must be used with astuteness,
    for love and loyalty are given to servant shepherds.

The more complex laws legislators make,
    the more ways people find around them.
The more rules are enacted or enforced by leaders,
    the poorer followers become.

The more frequently force is used by leaders,
    the more violence is tolerated.
The more shepherds value cunning and cleverness,
    the more deceitful followers become.

When leaders embrace inner quiet,
    followers discover the Way.
When shepherds maintain inner peace,
    followers seek tranquility.
When leaders do not meddle,
    followers experience success.
When shepherds eliminate countless desires,
    followers embrace simplicity.

      Before acting, reflect upon the value of inaction.

I BEG YOU TO SHEPHERD GOD'S FLOCK, FOR WHOM YOU ARE
RESPONSIBLE. WATCH OVER THEM BECAUSE YOU WANT TO, NOT
BECAUSE YOU ARE FORCED. THAT IS HOW GOD WANTS IT.
(I Peter 5:1–2 [NCV]).

Lead with Integrity

Jesus gave radical advice to leaders: "You know that those
who are regarded as rulers of the Gentiles lord it over them, and
their high officials exercise authority over them. Not so with you.
Instead, whoever wants to become great among you must be your
servant, and whoever wants to be first must be slave of all" (Mark
10:42–44). Leaders who practice the Way are to be servants of
those they lead.

This servant orientation is part of a larger moral vision in
which the best government is one in which people are given the
most freedom possible, and leaders practice the maximum amount
of self-restrained servanthood. Such leadership is willing to wait.
It trusts followers. Such leadership empowers followers. It allows
them the experience of success and failure. Wise leaders ponder
the benefits of acting and of doing nothing. Leaders of the Way
avoid conflict and seek peace. This kind of leadership develops the
capacities and confidence of those they lead.

What are some of the important characteristics of a virtuous leader?
Why is restraint so important in a leader? What can followers do to encourage
wisdom in leaders?

CHAPTER 58

When leadership is quiet and self-effacing,
    followers attain wholeness with minimal help.
When a shepherd becomes too active,
    followers rely upon the leader and become lazy.
When a leader becomes too controlling,
    followers who disagree become deceitful.

Failure often breeds later success,
    and success often breeds ultimate failure.
Good things often change into bad things,
    and bad things often turn out for good.
Who knows the precise result of any action?

The wise shepherd considers many alternatives,
    and chooses a path of minimal disruption.
This principle is difficult to grasp—
    yet it characterizes the Way.

Be energetic at the proper moment.
Be diligent but careful in action.

      Wait on the Word.
      Seek the Deep Light
      Follow the Way.
      Act in Deep Love.

WHEN HIS FATHER-IN-LAW SAW ALL THE WORK MOSES WAS DOING,
HE SAID, "WHY ARE YOU CONSTANTLY OVERWORKING? WHY DO
YOU SIT ALONE SURROUNDED BY PEOPLE FROM MORNING TILL
EVENING? THIS IS NOT SMART. YOU AND THE PEOPLE ARE SIMPLY
WEARING YOURSELVES OUT. WE NEED TO GET YOU SOME HELP!"
(Exodus 18:14–17 [author's paraphrase])

Lead Without Controlling

The best leaders are characterized by restraint. Leaders who
over-control followers and enact many complicated and subtle laws
breed confusion and chaos. Instead of producing virtue, such leaders
make people devious and dishonest. The result is contentiousness.

Above all, wise leaders remember their limitations. Wise public
service involves a balancing act, in which confusion and complexity
are potential aspects of whatever is done. The only way they can be
avoided is through wise restraint. Organizational restraint cannot
be achieved unless leaders learn the value and discipline of self-
restraint. Leaders need to be energetic. But, they must act wisely
not to waste energy, their own energy or that of their followers.
This involves learning the importance of self-knowledge and self-
management. In this way, social harmony can be achieved.

*Can you think of a time when you faced success and/or failure? How did
success and failure mold your character? What one aspect of your character do
you think you most need to manage?*

Chapter 59

Simplicity,
Self-control,
Sacrificial love:

These are central to following the Way.
Leaders of the Way embody these virtues.

Shepherds who diligently follow the Way from youth
    have virtue sufficient for their task.
When a leader has sufficient virtue,
    all that is wise can be accomplished.
Focus on achieving wise character;
    then success in necessary duties is possible.

When you know the Word and follow the Way
    your actions will be wise, and
        your leadership will endure.

Be deeply rooted in the Word.
Grow strong by following the Way.

In this way, long life and a vision of eternity are achieved.

TRUST IN THE LORD WITH ALL OF YOUR HEART, AND DO NOT RELY
ON YOUR OWN INSIGHT. IN ALL YOUR WAYS ACKNOWLEDGE HIM,
AND HE WILL MAKE STRAIGHT YOUR PATHS.
(Proverbs 3:5–6 [NRSV])

Be Simple, Self-Controlled, and Sacrificial

We expect leaders to live in large houses and wear fine and expensive clothes. We want our President, for example, to look "Presidential." We encourage leaders to be "celebrities". Scripture and the *Tao Te Ching* encourage a radically different expectation. Wisdom encourages us to seek leaders who have slowly and quietly become simple, self-controlled and sacrificial.

The best leaders are frugal and so conserve their strength. They are moderate in their desires. They possess self control. Jesus said, "For he who is the least among you all—he is the greatest" (Luke 9:48). The best leaders are self-effacing servant leaders who seek to serve the needs of followers. They are not afraid to "stand under" those they serve. This kind of leadership is rare in a narcissistic society that constantly promotes a "cult of personality". Yet, people who are able to slowly develop a servant character find the secret of true leadership and they joy of eternal life as well.

*What kind of preparation is most important for success
in leading others? In what ways do you exercise leadership?
What life experiences prepared you to lead others? Of the virtues of simplicity,
self-control and love, which do you most need to develop?*

CHAPTER 60

Leading others requires experience and skill—
    shepherding others is like cooking fresh trout
        over a small camp fire
           beside a mountain stream.
In order to achieve the best results,
    act wisely and do not overdo,
    act carefully and do no damage,
    act with balance and you will not fail.

When shepherding others, follow the Way—
    the Powers and Principalities are restrained.
Yet, the potential for chaos and evil always remains,
    so a leader must remain cautious.

Wise leaders shun violence and conflict,
    seeking harmony in every act and decision.

This is the way of wise, nonviolent peaceableness:

        Deep Light reveals the Way.
        Deep Love overcomes disorder.
        Conflict is avoided.
        Harmony is restored.

FINALLY, BE STRONG IN THE LORD AND IN THE STRENGTH OF HIS POWER. PUT ON THE WHOLE ARMOR OF GOD, SO THAT YOU MAY BE ABLE TO STAND AGAINST THE WILES OF THE DEVIL. FOR OUR STRUGGLE IS NOT AGAINST ENEMIES OF BLOOD AND FLESH, BUT AGAINST THE RULERS, AGAINST THE AUTHORITIES, AGAINST THE COSMIC POWERS OF THIS PRESENT DARKNESS, AGAINST THE SPIRITUAL FORCES OF EVIL IN THE HEAVENLY PLACES.

(Ephesians 6:10–12 [NRSV])

Retain Balance in the Face of Powers

Paul speaks of rulers, authorities, powers and principalities— embodiments of spiritual powers by which the world is ruled (Ephesians 6:12). Often, we think that if only we had power, we would lead others differently, only to find that we too come under the sway of pride and lust for power. When in leadership, we develop the same qualities we disliked in others. We too fall under the sway of the powers and principalities.

The Tao teaches that spiritual leadership requires the kind of simplicity required to "cook small fish over a fire." The wise leader thinks and acts with insight, humility, balance and restraint, and so disarms the powers and principalities as much as possible. This is the Way of the servant leader who models himself or herself after Christ.

There is an invisible realm of spiritual powers embodied in people and institutions. These powers can harm society and people. Can wise leaders disarm these powers? In your opinion, how can this accomplished? Can it be fully accomplished?

CHAPTER 61

Wise leaders know the power of humility.
Power flows to and from servanthood,
    as water softly flows into nearby marshland.
Servanthood embraces Deep Light.
Servanthood embodies Deep Love.

Tranquility in the exercise of power
    gives rise to successful leadership.
If you are like a fertile valley,
    growth and new life will come to followers.

If you are already powerful,
    humility increases your effectiveness.
If you are in a humble position,
    servanthood lifts you up.
Influence flows toward a modest nature.

Leaders of many should protect and help many;
    leaders of few should protect and help few—
        then, and only then, will harmony prevail
        and Deep Peace emerge.

This is the way of the Servant Shepherd.

In this world kings and great men order their people around, and yet they are called "friends of the people." But among you, those who are the greatest should take the lowest rank, and the leader should be like a servant.
(Luke 22:25–26 [NLT])

Understand the Power of Humble Servanthood

Although there is an active component to leadership, there is also a passive element. The Tao uses the metaphor of "the female" to describe the ability to overcome difficult circumstances with stillness and receptivity. The *Bible* teaches that wise leaders understand that personal humility and a servant spirit are important to solving problems. This involves being willing to stand below followers, and so serve them and their best interests.

When leaders place the search for wise solutions before personal recognition, followers profit. This kind of leadership is characterized by respect and love for those being led and their hopes and needs. By leading in this manner, wise leaders promote personal growth among followers. They are not afraid to wait in receptive anticipation for events to unfold. When a person is able to bring this leadership to a situation, whether large or small, there is harmony. Interestingly enough, power tends to flow towards, not away from, this kind of person.

Do you consider servanthood, tranquility, and humility essential to wise leadership? Why or why not? Do you struggle with humility? Why?

CHAPTER 62

The Word is a treasure chest of Deep Light
 for the righteous, a refuge for those who fall away.

Never abandon those who leave the Way;
 the wise are known by words of caution
  and by acts of healing care.
Such words and deeds heal the lost wanderer.

Follow the path of righteous people—
 the Spirit will help you become righteous.
Follow the path of wise people—
 the Spirit will help you achieve wisdom.

Wise counsel is of great value to a wise shepherd.
Honor leaders with wise counsel—
 flattery is of no value to anyone.
The Word and the Way are of eternal value.

Why was the Way esteemed by followers of the Word
 from the most ancient times?
Following the Way we find Mercy and Forgiveness.
Is it not said: "Mercy triumphs over judgment"?

This is the power of Deep Love.

WHICH ONE OF YOU, HAVING A HUNDRED SHEEP AND LOSING ONE
OF THEM, DOES NOT LEAVE THE NINETY-NINE IN THE WILDERNESS
AND GO AFTER THE ONE WHO IS LOST UNTIL HE FINDS IT? WHEN
HE HAS FOUND IT, HE LAYS IT ON HIS SHOULDERS AND REJOICES.
(Luke 15:4 [NRSV])

Rescue the Lost and Foolish

The Way is for everyone, not just for leaders. The wise follow the Way, are protected by God, and prosper. One of the primary goals of wisdom literature is that simple people may become wise (See Proverbs 1:2–6). Even simple people who follow the Way become wise. After faith, hope and love, what one thing can we give our families, coworkers, friends, and leaders that will contribute most to their happiness and wholeness? Wisdom!

Sometimes, giving wisdom means having compassion on those lost in error and foolishness. The wise person never abandons the simple but rescues them from their foolishness by encouraging wisdom and practicing mercy. The greatest gift we can receive is the gift of forgiveness and mercy. The greatest gift we can give others is to show them forgiveness and mercy and the Way to the source of forgiveness and mercy—to find them when they are lost.

If you were a leader, which would you value most: wise counsel or luxurious gifts? Why is good counsel the most important gift we can give another? Can you think of a time you gave another person the gift of good advice? How did they react?

Chapter 63

Deep Light and Deep Love are the act and being
    of the One Who Is and Will Be.

Embrace simplicity:

> Be willing to take no action at all.
> Act with grace in the least exertion.
> Greatness is achieved by small actions.
> Remain alert and humble.

When simple people and fools give unrestrained praise,
    look for trouble to come sooner than you expect.
When a task seems easy,
    look for hidden complications.
A wise leader anticipates difficulties,
    and then, the task is easier than expected.

Do simple things before difficult things.
Solve difficult problems before they become demanding.
Begin vast undertakings with simple and easy steps.
Never take on more than you can achieve.
Undertake only what is required.
Leave nothing necessary undone.

Trust the Grace of the One Who Is.

SUPPOSE ONE OF YOU WANTS TO BUILD A TOWER. WILL HE
NOT FIRST SIT DOWN AND ESTIMATE THE COST TO SEE IF HE
HAS ENOUGH MONEY TO COMPLETE IT? FOR IF HE LAYS THE
FOUNDATION AND IS NOT ABLE TO FINISH IT, EVERYONE WHO SEES
IT WILL RIDICULE HIM SAYING, "THIS FELLOW BEGAN TO BUILD AND
WAS NOT ABLE TO FINISH."
(Luke 14:28–30 [NIV])

Achieve Greatness by Doing Small Things

Most of us have heard our parents say, "Never procrastinate."
Wise people act while problems are small and the effort required
to solve them is moderate. Too often, people delay addressing
difficulties and then seek dramatic, costly solutions to complicated
problems. So, wise leaders attack problems when they are small and
more easily solved.

The best course of action is to take early, small steps to make
a problem smaller, thus solving it over time. Grandiose solutions
usually reflect unbounded pride and an overestimation of what our
limited, human abilities can achieve. Smaller solutions are generally
harder to develop, but they create lasting benefits. In addition, they
are less likely to have unforeseen, negative consequences.

*"Greatness lies in small things." What kinds of small things in your life could
have great results? Why is procrastination a character defect? Can you think of
a time when a leader would have been better served to seek a timely but small
solution to a problem before it became unmanageable?*

CHAPTER 64

Events are easier to manage in tranquil times.
Avert trouble before it begins.
Take action before things get out of hand.
Small problems are easily overcome.
Objectives gained ruthlessly slip away.
Fragile things break easily.
A tall tree begins with a small seed.
A tower begins with a deep foundation.
A great journey begins with one stride.

Hasty action brings failure.
Possessions grasped too tightly are lost.
A wise leader patiently allows events to unfold.

Wisdom may be found by anyone if he or she will:

> Trust the Word.
> Follow the Way.
> Adapt to Reality.

Do not be anxious; anxiety breeds failure.
Give up illusory gain; seek genuine success.
Seek nothing; receive everything.
Value Deep Light and Deep Love.
Bring Deep Peace and harmony to the world.

THE KINGDOM OF HEAVEN IS LIKE A MUSTARD SEED THAT SOMEONE
TOOK AND SOWED IN HIS FIELD; IT IS THE SMALLEST OF ALL THE
SEEDS, BUT WHEN IT HAS GROWN IT IS THE GREATEST OF SHRUBS
AND BECOMES A TREE, SO THAT THE BIRDS OF THE AIR COME AND
MAKE NESTS IN ITS BRANCHES.
(Matthew 13:31–32 [NRSV])

Timeliness in Action Is Important

We live in a culture that values action. To many in the East,
the West seems overly-hasty and impatient. There is a time to act
and a way to act, and there is a time not to act, allowing events
to unfold like a seed growing silently in the earth. Passion often
results in impulsivity premature action. Premature action often
causes even greater difficulties. Therefore, a wise person acts at the
proper time.

This is not an excuse for delay. A wise person does not act
when he or she lacks understanding. But, a wise person always
avoids procrastination. The best time to solve a problem is when it
is small. Most problems do not become easier to solve over time.
They become more difficult to solve. The wise leader, therefore,
learns when and where to take the smallest action to avoid the
largest problem. The wise leader learns to "plant the tiny seed" of
a solution and patiently watch it grow.

*Why is waiting an important discipline to practice? How does patience overcome
anxiety? Can you think of times when you acted from worry or anxiety when
waiting would have been a better course of action?*

CHAPTER 65

Two things are necessary to embrace Deep Light:

> Learn the Path of Wisdom.
> Unlearn the Path of Foolishness.

Clever leaders ultimately create disorder.
Where people are merely clever, honesty is rare;
    dishonesty, violence, and chaos reign.

Wise leaders display the simplicity of the Way.
Simplicity leads to progress.
The people learn deep wisdom
    and become virtuous and prosperous.

A wise leader avoids mere cleverness
    and chooses the Way.

Deep wisdom is profound.
When natural instincts return to the Way,
    divine and human harmony is restored.

This is the power of Deep Love and Deep Light.

THE WAYS OF RIGHT-LIVING PEOPLE GLOW WITH LIGHT; THE LONGER THEY LIVE, THE BRIGHTER THEY SHINE. BUT THE ROAD OF WRONGDOING GETS DARKER AND DARKER—TRAVELERS CAN'T SEE A THING; THEY FALL FLAT ON THEIR FACES.
(Proverbs 4:18–19 [Message])

Unlearn Foolish Habits

To understand the deeper meaning of the Way, one begins by distinguishing the kind of knowledge that leads to wisdom from a kind of knowledge that leads only to shrewdness or cleverness. The Apostle Paul urges the Colossians to avoid "vain philosophy and deceit" (Colossians 2:8). This is the kind of knowledge true wisdom discourages: a mere shrewdness that has lost its connection with a deeper rationality, what in the West we might call "Natural Law."

The deepest wisdom is for everyone and goes beyond personal or group advantage. Leading people to virtue is much more difficult than leading them to embrace an immediate course of action. To become this kind of leader requires that leaders unlearn beliefs and habits that are unwise. They must learn to look beyond temporary advantage in order to truly improve the lives of others. It is important that true servant leaders seek this deeper wisdom in managing people and situations.

What is the difference between a wise leader and a clever leader? Why is cleverness so often a fatal quality in a person or leader? Can you think of times when you were merely clever as opposed to wise, and it backfired on you?

CHAPTER 66

Rivers are greater than mountain streams;
    lying below, they are filled by rushing waters.
Similarly, if you want to shepherd people,
    you must place your interests below theirs.
You will be filled with the rushing waters of Deep Love.

The paradox of leadership is this:

    To lead, you must be willing to follow.
    To shepherd, you must be willing to be a sheep.
    To stand above, you must be willing to stand under.

A wise shepherd does not burden followers.
The best leader serves others with humility and grace.

It is better to shepherd followers towards virtue
    than to manipulate them toward a transient goal.
The world eventually praises such leaders,
    and the joy of their success never fades.

A wise leader does not unnecessarily contend with others.
No one can compare with such a shepherd.

ENDOW THE KING WITH YOUR JUSTICE, O GOD, THE ROYAL
SON WITH YOUR RIGHTEOUSNESS. HE WILL JUDGE YOUR PEOPLE
IN RIGHTEOUSNESS, YOUR AFFLICTED ONES WITH JUSTICE. THE
MOUNTAINS WILL BRING PROSPERITY TO THE PEOPLE, THE HILLS
THE FRUIT OF RIGHTEOUSNESS.
(Psalm 72:1–3 [NIV])

Leaders Must Also Follow

Christian commentators often call Jesus the first, great exemplar
of servant leadership. Jesus placed his interests below that of his
followers. He was willing to die for them. Among contemporary
leaders, "servant leadership" often becomes a devious tradeoff: "I
pretend to give you what you want, and you place me in power." "I
pretend to care about your needs and you allow me to lead." This is
not true servant leadership; it is deceitfulness and manipulation.

True servant leadership seeks the good of followers before the
good of the leader. Such leaders are honest with followers and
do not mislead them. They rely on common sense and wisdom
rather than cleverness and manipulation. The key to this kind of
leadership lies in what kind of person we *are* not in what we *do*.
Slowly, surely, gently by the power of the Spirit, authority flows to
such leaders.

*What does it mean to put the interests of followers above that of a leader? What
difference would it make in your life if you put the interests of others above
your interests?*

CHAPTER 67

Worldly people merely say they honor the Way.
Hypocrites merely give the Word lip service.
Most people only praise the Word with their tongues;
    they do not follow the Way from their hearts.

Maintain three virtues of the Way—
    they are pearls of great value:

        Deep Love,
        Moderate Simplicity,
        Great Humility.

Deep Love avoids self-centeredness—
    producing sacrifice for the betterment of others.
Simplicity and moderation avoid excessive spending—
    producing generosity to those in need.
Humility avoids pride—
    producing empathy with the all people.

Courage without Deep Love becomes violent.
Generosity without simplicity becomes showing off.
Pretending to be humble while in leadership
    leads to hypocrisy and manipulation.

To save or set free a person or a people
    the Word rescues by means of Deep Love.

BE OF THE SAME MIND TOWARD ONE ANOTHER. DO NOT SET YOUR MIND ON HIGH THINGS, BUT ASSOCIATE WITH THE HUMBLE. DO NOT BE WISE IN YOUR OWN OPINION. REPAY NO ONE EVIL FOR EVIL. (Romans 12:16 [NKJV])

To Save Others, Practice Deep Love

For Christians, the root virtues are faith, hope, and love. Faith is trust in God, even when answers are delayed. Hope clings to the promises of God, even when discouraged. Selfless, sacrificial love does what is best for others, even when suffering results. Sacrificial love crowns the character of a great servant leader, because sacrificial love empowers a leader to embrace doing what is best for others whatever the cost.

In this chapter, the *Tao Te Ching* takes us to the root of the Taoist ethic: the virtues of compassion, simplicity, and humility. Deep love involves compassion for all things and people. Simplicity involves contentment with having one's needs satisfied, as opposed to the never-ending "wants" we all experience. Humility involves recognizing our common humanity and not thinking oneself better than others. These virtues ennoble leaders and followers alike. When we develop love, simplicity and humility we are able to set aside our selfish desires and meet the needs of others.

The three great virtues of Taoism are deep love, simplicity, and humility. Christianity values each of these as well. Why do you suppose that Lao Tzu chose these three? What three virtues would you chose as most important to a wise life? Why is love the most important virtue in a servant leader?

135

Chapter 68

Wise leaders serve followers as gentle shepherds.
Whenever possible, wise shepherds seek
    peace and harmony in human relationships.

The Word brings wisdom by Deep Light.
The Way is found in Deep Love.
Deep Love produces harmony and peace.

Wise leaders shun violence and conflict.
This is the virtue of avoiding violence and conflict—
    the ability to manage people and situations
        as gently as snow falls in winter.

The best policy is this:
    Avoid conflict if at all possible.
If conflict arises, the best policy is this:
    Avoid unnecessary destruction.
If conflict continues, the best policy is this:
    Seek a just solution.
If conflict reaches a conclusion, the best policy is this:
    Show mercy and restore good relations.

This is the Way.

BLESSED ARE THE PEACEMAKERS, FOR THEY WILL BE CALLED
CHILDREN OF GOD.
(Matthew 5:9 [NRSV])

The Best Leaders Avoid Conflict

Conflict and violence are, unfortunately, part of the human condition. They cannot be entirely avoided. Therefore, those who must engage in conflict need to exhibit emotional and physical restraint. In this, following the Way involves something like "the strategy of the indirect approach" promoted by military theoreticians: Defuse opposition by careful planning before overt conflict even begins.

The wise leader avoids conflict, preferring to create circumstances in which an objective can be obtained without argument or violence. Even when necessary, force should never be unrestrained or motivated by anger or fear. By avoiding conflict as much as possible, a wise leader serves the deeper needs of people. By restraint, a wise leader causes as little damage as possible. For Christian-Followers, the principle of minimizing conflict is crucial. It is not enough for Christians to be wise toward an enemy during conflict. Christ-Followers must also love and pray for enemies. They must take risks to minimize harm, even to enemies. This is harder than mere self-control and self-restraint.

In your opinion, when is conflict to be avoided and when accepted? Can you think of a time when you were drawn into an unnecessary conflict? How could you have handled the situation differently?

CHAPTER 69

Wise shepherds understand this truth:

The Word does not favor an aggressor.
Violence undoes the stability and peace of the Word.

It is better to be attacked and trust the One Who Is
    than to attack and find a temporary victory.

To avoid conflict:

Advance your interests without using force.
Confront without overtly clashing.
Use the indirect approach.

Never underestimate your adversary;
    one who underestimates an opponent
        squanders every advantage.

Never overestimate your adversary;
    one who overestimates an opponent
        squanders every opportunity for achievement.

When there is disagreement,
    success often comes to those who avoid conflict.

Therefore, the wise seek a peaceful result.

[W]HAT KING GOING OUT TO WAR AGAINST ANOTHER KING, WILL
NOT SIT DOWN FIRST AND CONSIDER WHETHER HE IS ABLE WITH
TEN THOUSAND TO OPPOSE THE ONE WHO COMES AGAINST HIM
WITH TWENTY THOUSAND? IF HE CANNOT, THEN, WHILE THE
OTHER IS STILL FAR AWAY, HE SENDS A DELEGATION AND ASKS FOR
THE TERMS OF PEACE.
(Luke 14:31–32 [NRSV])

Never Underestimate an Adversary

Often, the *Tao Te Ching* is read as recommending classic pacifism.
This is a mistaken reading, as passages that involve war indicate.
However, Lao Tzu plainly considers war a calamity. Conflict is to
be avoided, and if conflict is necessary, the wise leader moderates
it as much as possible.

Conflict involves many uncertainties. Many conflicts and
defeats come from underestimating or overestimating the strength
of an opponent. Therefore, the wise leader makes every effort to
avoid conflict and is drawn into conflict only when all reasonable
alternatives are exhausted. If conflict erupts, it is best to use indirect
methods to achieve an end rather than direct methods of conflict.
If action must be taken, however, the wise leader acts with vigor.
When the conflict is over, a wise leader acts with grace to diffuse
hard feelings as much as possible.

*Strategists sometimes talk of the "strategy of the indirect approach." Think of a
current or past conflict in your life. What would it mean or have meant to use a
more indirect means to resolve the conflict?*

CHAPTER 70

The Way is easy to understand and can be followed
  if the Word is present by the Spirit.
Without the Spirit, no one can understand the Word,
  nor can anyone follow the Way without grace.

Those who are able to embody the Word are few.
Those who are able to follow the Way are rare.

Deep Light streams from the Word.
Deep Love creates healthy relationships.
The Way is the Way of Deep Love.

The source of the Way is the Word;
  following this Way results in wise action.
Those who do not know the Word and its tradition
  cannot understand the Way—much less follow it.

The wise value the Word and the Way.
Such persons are like precious jewels hidden in a field.

Most people miss deep inner loveliness,
  like beauty hidden under a coarse garment.
The loveliness of the Word and the Way
  can only be seen by the Deep Light.
The beauty of the Word and the Way
  is only revealed by Deep Love.

COME TO ME, ALL YOU WHO ARE WEARY AND BURDENED, AND I
WILL GIVE YOU REST. TAKE MY YOKE UPON YOU AND LEARN FROM
ME, FOR I AM GENTLE AND HUMBLE IN HEART, AND YOU WILL FIND
REST FOR YOUR SOULS.
(Matthew 11:28–29 [NIV])

Understand and Follow the Difficult Way

If the virtues of deep love, simplicity, and humility are so obvious and the benefits so clear, why is it we have so much difficulty adopting them? The Apostle John speaks of the hidden, easily missed wisdom of God. "The true light that gives light to every man was coming into the world. He was in the world, and though the world was made through him, the world did not recognize him" (John 1:9–10).

The Way of Wisdom is easy to understand but hard to put into practice because it contradicts not only our clouded reason but also our deepest human desires. The path of wisdom looks easy, but it is in fact very difficult to put into practice because it involves both self-knowledge and self-control. The wise person undertakes to develop self-knowledge and the virtues of the wise life, and then undertakes the difficult process of self-control that makes wise living possible. This is a long, but blessed process.

Why does the world sometimes miss the value of wisdom? In what ways do you need to know yourself better than you do? In what ways to your natural desires and human anxieties prevent you from living wisely?

Chapter 71

Even among the wise, knowledge is partial and imperfect,
    and ignorance vast and deep as the ocean depths.
The wise as well as the foolish can flounder
    in the tumult of the pounding waves of ignorance.

No person fully understands the mind of the One Who Is.

The humble people know these things:

    Reality is subtle and beyond our full understanding.
    Wisdom is elusive and difficult to attain.
    Error is difficult to uncover but easy to commit.

Straying from the Way is a constant danger—
    for the Way is narrow and easily lost.
Only by grace can one follow the Way.

Pride of heart is a fatal disease and brings suffering.
Sensible people recognize pride is an illness
    and are cured of its fever.

Wise people understand this:

    Cautiously attain watchful tranquility:
    Remain Centered and watch quietly
        until the Deep Light is revealed.

EXPERIENCE USES FEW WORDS; DISCERNMENT KEEPS A COOL HEAD.
EVEN A FOOL, IF HE KEEPS HIS MOUTH SHUT, WILL SEEM WISE; IF HE
HOLDS HIS TONGUE HE WILL SEEM INTELLIGENT.
(Proverbs 17:27–28 [REV])

Know Yourself and Your Limits

It is impossible for us to manage our emotions and our reactions
if we do not understand them. It is impossible to act wisely if
we do not know our limitations. Socrates, the Greek philosopher,
said, "Know thyself." John Calvin, the great Reformer, classified
all knowledge into two parts: knowledge of self and of God. Wise
people have self-understanding: they understand how much they do
not know as well as the limits on what they know and can do. They
possess emotional self-understanding and self-control.

When we are wise, we do not constantly show others how
much we know, nor are we constantly deceiving others concerning
what we do and do not know. Because we have developed true
humility, we possess open and teachable spirits. Leadership books
often speak of great leaders as first achieving self-understanding
and self-management. This flows from the kind of self-knowledge
that creates a teachable spirit. This teachable spirit is necessary for
self understanding and to understand others.

*How would your life change if you reflected regularly upon how much you don't
know? How do you think you are doing in the areas of self-knowledge and self-
management?*

CHAPTER 72

When people do not fear harmful things,
    dark adversity descends upon the land.
Decadence is never far from the arrogant.
Failure is never far from the proud—
    the One Who Is and Will Be opposes them.

Never unnecessarily reduce the income of citizens
    or oppress the poor or working people.
Such behavior is great foolishness in a leader.

Wise leaders have self-understanding—
    without unwarranted meekness or burning pride.
Wise leaders have self-control—
    without rigidity or unbending self-righteousness.
Wise shepherds are forceful—
    without resorting to aggressive violence.
Wise shepherds lead by Deep Light in Deep Love.

If you love yourself without conceit—
    if you love others without restraint—
    if you love the One Who Is without limit—
      you have the wisdom to lead others.

SPEAK UP FOR THOSE WHO CANNOT SPEAK FOR THEMSELVES, FOR
THE RIGHTS OF ALL WHO ARE DESTITUTE. SPEAK UP AND JUDGE
FAIRLY; DEFEND THE RIGHTS OF THE POOR AND NEEDY.
(Proverbs 31:8-9 [NIV])

Care for the Poor and Weak

During times of success, people often become proud and lose their sense of limits. They forget to care for the poor and weak. In times of decadence, people lose a sense of what constitutes dreadful or immoral activity. In times of tranquility, people lose a sense of the fragility of peace. When these things happen, terrible suffering can result. The wise person maintains his or her conscience and an appreciation for the potential for suffering when the Way is violated. In this way, wise leaders promote social harmony.

Wise shepherds recognize the fragility of social peace and refrain from taking advantage of those entrusted to their care. Good leaders care for all people, especially the poor and helpless. When Jesus saw the crowds, "he had compassion on them, because they were harassed and helpless, like sheep without a shepherd" (Matthew 9:36). Humble servant leaders avoid pride. This permits them a compassionate heart that identifies with, and responds to, the needs of others especially the poor and oppressed.

In what ways do you show a love for the poor in your life? How would you be wiser if you did show this love for poorer people? How could you find ways to relate to the poor and rejected of your community in a useful, helpful, and healthy way?

CHAPTER 73

Humility enables Deep Light to illuminate the Way.
Caution born of wisdom avoids fatal mistakes.
Compassion born of Deep Love avoids destructive conflict.

Overconfidence is deadly in a leader.
Audacity leads to overreaching and failure.
Prudence leads to success.

Followers of the Way
    do not contend with others for recognition.
Followers of the Way
    achieve their objectives in Deep Love.

Wisdom prepares for difficult circumstances
    yet is without anxiety.
Wisdom does not need to speak constantly
    yet responds appropriately.
Wisdom awaits the proper moment to proceed
    and so acts without unnecessary struggle.

No human being fully knows or determines the future;
    and no leader fully controls future events.

The future is in the hands of the One Who Is and Will Be.
The net of the Word is made with wide mesh.
Those who are led by the Spirit abide within the Way.
They experience the peace of Heaven.

COMMIT YOUR WORK TO THE LORD, AND YOUR PLANS WILL BE
ESTABLISHED. THE LORD HAS MADE EVERYTHING FOR ITS PURPOSE,
EVEN THE WICKED FOR THE DAY OF TROUBLE. ALL THOSE WHO ARE
ARROGANT ARE AN ABOMINATION TO THE LORD; BE ASSURED, THEY
WILL NOT GO UNPUNISHED.
(Proverbs 16:3–5 [NRSV])

Caution Is a Virtue in a Leader

There is a kind of audacity that emulates courage but is really
imprudent foolishness. It masquerades as courage. But, events reveal
it to be foolhardiness. The author of Proverbs writes, "It is not
good to have zeal without knowledge, nor be hasty and miss the
way" (Proverbs 19:2). People of the Way develop wise fortitude.

Wisdom acts with caution and deliberation. This is especially
important in a leader, whose actions can affect many people.
Wisdom counts the cost of alternative courses of action and
weighs carefully the risks and benefits of alternatives. Wisdom
prefers a victory won by strategy to a victory won by force. Above
all, wisdom is patient, allowing circumstances to develop and reveal
the wise course of action. Respecting the deep wisdom of the
universe, a wise person acts with patient circumspection, especially
in difficult or dangerous circumstances.

*Can you think of a time when you were overconfident and acted impulsively?
What was the result? What does it mean to act with caution, care, and
compassion?*

CHAPTER 74

Wise shepherds do not expect
    punishment, even capital punishment,
        to produce virtue in people.
Fear of punishment or death deters violence
    only when people anticipate consequences.
Most people do not anticipate harm or death;
    they fail to number their days.
Therefore, fear of punishment or death
    is of limited use in producing social harmony.

The wise shepherd recognizes this:
    Judgment belongs to the One Who Is and Will Be.
Usurping the work of the Word accomplishes nothing.
Playing executioner is a waste of energy and time.

Therefore, a wise shepherd understands
    the foolishness of relying on excessive punishment.

Punishment is not the best Way of the Servant Shepherd.

THEY SAID TO JESUS, "THIS WOMAN WAS CAUGHT IN THE ACT OF
ADULTERY. SHALL WE STONE HER?" JESUS KNEELED AND WROTE IN
THE DUST. THEN HE STOOD UP AND SAID, "LET THE ONE WITHOUT
SIN THROW THE FIRST STONE!" WHEN THEY HEARD HIM, THEY
DEPARTED UNTIL ONLY JESUS WAS LEFT. THEN HE SAID TO THE
WOMAN, "WHERE ARE YOUR ACCUSERS? DID NOT EVEN ONE OF
THEM CONDEMN YOU?" "NO, LORD," SHE SAID. SO, JESUS SAID,
"NEITHER DO I. GO AND SIN NO MORE."

(John 8:4–11 [Author's paraphrase])

Let Heaven Judge

The *Tao Te Ching* counsels that many violent crimes are
committed by those who do not fear punishment. The cure for
violence ultimately lies elsewhere—in the conversion of the human
spirit from a love of violence to peaceableness, from passion to
reason.

Wisdom counsels leaders not to place too much confidence in
punishment as a source of social harmony. In the end, judgment
is best left to the Ultimate Lawgiver. When we play God toward
others, we step out of our proper role as created creatures. As Jesus
put it, "Do not judge, or you too will be judged. For in the same
way you judge others, you will be judged, and with the measure you
use, it will be measured to you" (Matthew 7:1–2).

Do most criminals consider the punishment before committing a crime?
Do children consider punishment before they act in disobedient ways?
If fear of punishment fails to deter, what behaviors are most
likely to create obedient character?

CHAPTER 75

Wise people do not strive for more wealth
    than is needed and healthy.
Wise people value others as they value themselves.
This is the foundation of peace.

When leaders take too much from those they lead,
    ordinary people do not have enough.
This causes unrest and disorder—harmony is lost.

When shepherds restrain themselves and their desires,
    allowing the people to amass sufficient wealth,
        there is peace and order in the community.

When ordinary people are desperate and anxious
    and the rich have too much,
        there is dissatisfaction and rebellion.

When the ordinary people have enough
    and the rich do not have too much,
        harmony prevails and the land enjoys peace.

The Way of the Deep Love is a way of
    self-restraint and humble service to others.

THE RIGHTEOUS CARE ABOUT JUSTICE FOR THE POOR,
BUT THE WICKED HAVE NO SUCH CONCERN.
IF A KING JUDGES THE POOR WITH FAIRNESS,
HIS THRONE WILL ALWAYS BE SECURE.
(Proverbs 27:9; 7, 14 [NIV])

Do Not Usurp the Wealth of Others

Governments and the wealthy are always tempted to take too much of community wealth. There are limits to the projects that governments ought to undertake. There are limits to how much wealth governments ought to obtain. Excessive taxation is a source of dishonesty and social unrest. The Way urges wise restraint in government.

Private corporations and the wealthy must also practice moderation. Excessive concentration of wealth is a source of social tension. If the rich have too much, the poor will not have enough. Social harmony is produced by seeking a just balance in the distribution of wealth. Those who have power and wealth need to be restrained in the interests of everyone. Therefore, leaders seek to find ways to create a fair opportunity for the poor and average folks to achieve personal prosperity. When this is the case, everyone benefits.

What happens when leaders take too much of the national or communal wealth? How can wise leadership seek to support the needs of both the poor and the rich? What Christian principles should guide our thinking about the role and limitations of government?

CHAPTER 76

Plants are bendable and tender when alive
    but easily broken and dry when dead.
Animals are born soft and compliant, full of movement,
    but rigid and unbendable when dead.

Rigid and inflexible people are shattered by life;
Pliant and elastic people overcome difficulties.

Those who are stiff and rigid are easily defeated.
Those who are supple and elastic
    find success in almost every circumstance.

Therefore, students of the Word apply teaching wisely.
Followers of the Way adapt to changing circumstances.

Followers of the Way
    are willing to be illuminated by Deep Light
        and transformed by Deep Love.

This is the Path of Life.

Do not now be stiff-necked as your fathers were, but yield yourselves to the Lord and come to his sanctuary, which he has consecrated forever, and serve the Lord your God, that his fierce anger may turn away from you. For if you return to the Lord, your brothers and your children will find compassion with their captors and return to this land. For the Lord your God is gracious and merciful and will not turn away his face from you, if you return to him.
(2 Chronicles 30:8–9 [ESV])

Have a Teachable Heart

Flexibility and tenderness are characteristics of living things. People are born tender and flexible. As they grow older, they become stiff physically and set in their ways as a matter of character. The dead are stiff from *rigor mortis*.

The wise person avoids an inflexibility and hardness, restoring in the soul the characteristic flexibility of children. Developing the flexibility of the young is part of developing the kind of wisdom which permits the wise to see deeply into situations. Jesus puts it this way, "I tell you the truth, unless you change and become like little children, you will never enter the kingdom of heaven." (Matthew 18:3). Those who become like little children, with tender and teachable hearts, travel the Way of Christ.

Is your heart teachable or not? Are you a flexible or inflexible person? In what ways do you think it is contrary to wisdom to be unteachable or inflexible?

CHAPTER 77

The Way works in the world like a drawn bow:
    the top bends downward; the bottom bends up.
Create tension where there is none;
    reduce tension where it is too great.

    Concentrate.
    Achieve balance.
    Apply force slowly.
    Release calmly.

Greedy leaders take from those who have too little,
    while giving to those who have too much.

Followers of the Way take from their surplus and excess,
    providing for those who lack enough with open hearts.
This is the work of the Spirit of Generosity.

Who is able to give generously to the poor?
Those who follow the Way provide for the needy.
Wise followers of the Way give generously,
    expecting nothing in return.
They immediately forget their generosity,
    and do not seek praise for giving.

Those who seek to acquire too much
    bring suffering upon themselves and others.

Do not be afraid, little flock, for your Father has been pleased to give you the kingdom. Sell your possessions and give to the poor. Provide purses for yourselves that will not wear out, a treasure in heaven that will not be exhausted, where no thief comes near and no moth destroys. For where your treasure is, there your heart will be also.

(Luke 12:32–34 [NIV])

Be Generous on the Way

The *Tao Te Ching* has its own version of the "Doctrine of the Mean" (the view that the good exists between two extremes, i.e. bravery exists between foolhardiness and cowardice). As a bow creates tension when drawn, and the tension is released by reducing the draw, the wise know how to create tension and how to release tension. Foolish people create tension until a situation breaks or release tension so that nothing is accomplished.

The Spirit guides Christ-Follower in achieving a wise and loving balance among the tensions of life. One of the most difficult virtues for a Christ-Follower to develop are the virtues of contentment and generosity. It is hard for those attached to wealth to enter the kingdom of heaven (Mark 10:24–25), and we are all attached to our wealth. To be wise, we must overcome that attachment.

Do you consider generosity a virtue? Do you consciously restrict your consumption to give to your church, charities, and the poor? How would your life change if you sought to live more simply?

CHAPTER 78

Water is fluid and flows freely upon the earth,
    yet carves a deep valley through solid rock.
Over time, nothing can resist water—
    so it is with followers of the Way.

Gentle, constant and unending Deep Love
    overcomes inflexible rigidity and conflict.
Those who serve others, change others.
Resistance provokes resistance—
    it is better to turn the other cheek.
Only followers of the Word gently and peacefully
    put this knowledge into practice.

A wise shepherd knows this:
    A willing servant is worthy to lead.
    A humble servant is worthy to be exalted.
    Those who give are able to receive.
One who is willing to tackle unpleasant tasks
    is the best kind of leader.

The truest things in the world
    may only be understood as a paradox.
This is true of leadership:
    To lead wisely, serve well.

I TELL YOU NOT TO RESIST AN EVIL PERSON. BUT WHOEVER SLAPS YOU ON YOUR RIGHT CHEEK, TURN THE OTHER TO HIM ALSO. IF ANYONE WANTS TO SUE YOU AND TAKE AWAY YOUR TUNIC, LET HIM HAVE YOUR CLOAK ALSO. AND WHOEVER COMPELS YOU TO GO ONE MILE, GO WITH HIM TWO. GIVE TO HIM WHO ASKS YOU, AND FROM HIM WHO WANTS TO BORROW FROM YOU DO NOT TURN AWAY.
(Matthew 5:39–42 [NKJV])

To Change Others, Be Like Water

As anyone who has seen the Grand Canyon knows, water is soft and pliant, flowing where gravity takes it. But, over time, nothing can resist it. Water can carve a great canyon out of solid rock. So it is with those who are patient. The most difficult problems can be solved by long, slow, loving attention. The greatest disadvantage can be overcome over time.

The Psalmist cries out, "I waited patiently for the LORD; he turned to me and heard my cry. He lifted me out of the slimy pit, out of the mud and mire; he set my feet on a rock and gave me a firm place to stand" (Psalm 40:1–2). In an impatient culture, patience is a difficult virtue to acquire. But those who acquire the patient persistence of water are able to change the world.

Have you ever seen the Grand Canyon or any other great gorge? The Grand Canyon was carved by the power of water over centuries. How could you take a lesson from the way in which water works? How could you employ a gentle, unyielding force in seeking to lead others?

CHAPTER 79

When a conflict is over and peace has returned,
    hard feelings and desire for revenge may remain.
Violent conflict is, therefore, contrary to the Way,
    and should be avoided by wise leaders.

A wise shepherd does what justice requires,
    following the way of Deep Light.

A virtuous person does the proper thing
    under every circumstance.
Practitioners of Deep Love
    are even willing servants of adversaries.
Deep Love is even for enemies.

Persons without virtue take advantage of others
    and show no mercy to those in their debt.
This is not according to the Way.

Persons of the Way never take advantage of others
    and show mercy towards their debtors.
This is according to the Way.

Remember, the Word does not play favorites;
    it chooses no sides.

A righteous person is blessed by the Word
    because the Way is a path of blessing.

Happy are those who are hungry and thirsty for
goodness, for they will be fully satisfied! Happy are the
merciful, for they will have mercy shown to them!
(Matthew 5:6–7 [Phillips])

Be a Merciful Leader

Proverbs teaches, "A man's wisdom gives him patience; it is to his glory to overlook an offense" (Proverbs 19:11). Generally speaking, every solution to a problem creates new and unforeseen difficulties. Hurt and hard feelings are created during conflict, and it takes time, sometimes a lot of time, for these feelings to go away. Occasionally, a relationship is permanently injured by a disagreement. This is true even if the conflict was necessary and the best result obtained.

The wise person thinks clearly before entering into a dispute. When conflict erupts, a wise person works diligently to end it and eliminate hard feelings. Often, it is better to let another person have their way than to suffer the consequences of a dispute. It is also best not to dwell on mistakes of others or upon their weaknesses and wrongdoings. Mercy is the best source of interpersonal healing. Working on self-improvement, rather than on the improvement of others, is the best course of action.

After conflict, hard feelings often remain. Can you think of a situation in your life where this was true? Was the conflict worth it? How can one disagree with another person or even oppose that person in some way without undue hard feelings remaining?

CHAPTER 80

Even great and mighty nations, if they are wise,
    respect small communities and local customs.
Small communities do not seek, or even require,
    the weapons or tools of a great nation;
        and, if they are wise, they reject them.

Small communities posses a human size and scale.
Although they have technical knowledge,
    they employ technologies with a human scale.

Wise people do not impatiently stray away from their roots,
    nor do they restlessly move from place to place.
Those who value the wise life nurture a home place.

People with deep roots in their land and its customs
    delight in their own customs and traditions
        while respecting those of others.
Although another community is close by,
    wise people are content to grow old at home.

Enjoy food grown with your own hands.
Wear clothes made by your own hands.
Dwell in a home built with your own hands.
People who think small, evaluate matters wisely.
Those who value community, value wisely.

LIKE A BIRD THAT STRAYS FROM ITS NEST IS ONE WHO STRAYS
FROM HOME.
(Proverbs 27:8 [NRSV]).

Remember Small Is Beautiful

We live in a culture that exalts size and abundance of
possessions. The Tao exalts the small and the simple. We live in
a highly mobile culture in which few people have deep roots in a
community. The Tao exalts loyalty to a place, however humble. We
worship progress. The Tao urges respect for tradition. Wise people
respect small units, local traditions, and roots. Wise people are also
willing to cooperate where larger units of government or business
are needed to solve larger problems.

In the end, it is important to remember that contentment is
not born of size, possessions, wealth, or position. As Paul put it,
". . . godliness with contentment is great gain" (I Timothy 6:6–7).
The most important lesson of life is learning to be content with
what we have, with where we live, and with the cultural history we
inherited. This does not mean we do not seek to improve and make
better our inheritance. As Christ-Followers, we should. But, we
should also respect small things, local customs, and simple work.
The virtues of a wise leader are the virtues of a gardener: the soil
must be maintained as well as improved.

*People often worship size and visible success. What about you? Do you value
small things: family, home, community, and the simple pleasures of life? How
would your life change if you did?*

CHAPTER 81

True words are often course, not beautiful.
Beautiful sounding words are often untrue.
Wisdom does not come through smooth words.
The wise look beneath the surface
    into the heart and reality of situations.

The wise refrain from mere argument and debate.
Constant arguments are unproductive.
Only fools constantly argue and debate.

The wise are frequently not intellectuals,
    and intellectuals are frequently not wise.
Wisdom is the art of living astutely.

The wise need not amass vast wealth.
Serving the needs of others,
    the wise accumulate sufficient wealth.
The wise are generous to all people
    and blessed by true wealth.

A follower of the Way acts to benefit others.
Therefore, act to benefit everyone.
This is the true Way.

DEAR BROTHERS AND SISTERS, WHEN I FIRST CAME TO YOU I DID NOT USE LOFTY WORDS AND BRILLIANT IDEAS TO TELL YOU GOD'S MESSAGE. ... I CAME TO YOU IN WEAKNESS —TIMID AND TREMBLING. AND MY MESSAGE AND MY PREACHING WERE VERY PLAIN. I DID NOT USE WISE AND PERSUASIVE SPEECHES.... I DID THIS SO THAT YOU MIGHT TRUST THE POWER OF GOD RATHER THAN HUMAN WISDOM.
(I Corinthians 2:1, 4-5 [NLT])

Avoid Overly Sophisticated Arguments

The *Tao Te Ching* is a short work, and its style is rustic. The *Bible* is often simple and its writers simple, rustic people. Its writers were not always eloquent. Perhaps this was intentional.

The deepest truths often strike us as simplistic, childish, or unsophisticated. Sometimes, ideas that strike us as "adult, sophisticated, and deep" are in reality foolishness. This is what the Apostle Paul was speaking of when he said, "My message and my preaching were not with wise and persuasive words, but with a demonstration of the Spirit's power, so that your faith might not rest on men's wisdom, but on God's power" (I Corinthians 2:4–5). There is an Uncreated Wisdom deeper than human eloquence, a wisdom through which true happiness can be found.

Can you think if examples of fine words and sophisticated arguments leading you or those you love astray? Has this study helped you become more able to see beneath the superficial in life?

DEFINITIONS FOR SPECIFIC TERMS

The *Tao Te Ching*, the *Bible*, and Christian theology all use terms which may be unfamiliar to general readers. A few of these terms are clarified below:

DEEP LIGHT: The Apostle John teaches that "God is light," when he says, "This is the message we have heard from him and declare to you: God is light; in him there is no darkness at all" (I John 1:5). This Divine Light is the divine ground of reason, which existed before the created order. It is the "Logos," or Divine Reason immanent in the cosmos. In God, Divine Love and Divine Wisdom exist in harmony, so that love is not separated from wisdom. God's rationality never fails to act in love.

DEEP LOVE: In First John, the Apostle also teaches that, "God is love." John says, "Whoever does not love does not know God, because God is love" (I John 4:8). John goes on to define the nature of this Deep Love when he says, "This is how we know what love is, Jesus Christ laid down his life for us" (I John 3:16). Jesus says, "Greater love has no one than this, that he lay down his life for his friends" (John 15:13). The Divine Love, Deep Love of God, is a sacrificial, suffering love, which loves for the restoration, redemption, and renewal of the Beloved. It was revealed most clearly by Jesus Christ on the Cross.

ETERNAL: One area in which Taoism and Christianity differ concerns the notion of the Eternal. As used in the *Tao Te Ching*, the term refers to the unchanging, immanent order of the universe. It does not have divine connotations. The term "Eternal," as used in this work, means the Triune God revealed in the Old and New Testaments. In Exodus, when Moses asks God how to refer to God if the people of Israel ask, he answers, "I am who I am," which term can also be translated, I will be what I will be" (Exodus 3:14). In this paraphrase it is also used as a synonym for God, who is most often referred to as the "One Who Is" or the "One Who Is and Will Be." (See "One Who Is" below.)

FALSE SELF: The "False Self" is a construction of the human ego designed to project a more acceptable persona to others. This constructed False Self divides a person from the True Self, preventing psychological and spiritual wholeness. The human propensity to create a "False Self" is a coping mechanism resulting from our sense of insecurity and inadequacy, usually stemming from the anxieties of childhood, youth, and adolescence. From a religious perspective, our false self ultimately derives from our alienation from God and from God's creation due to pride and selfishness, our unwillingness to accept who God has made us, and our failure to recognize God's ultimate trustworthiness to redeem and bless us as creatures and the creation God made.

HEAVEN: For the Chinese, "Heaven" and the "Way of Heaven" do not have the supernatural connotations that those phrases have for Christians. In this adaptation, the term "Heaven" has a meaning close to what Jesus meant when he said that, by his incarnation, "the Kingdom of Heaven has come upon you." In Christ, the "shalom" (peace) of God, a state in which everything is where it belongs, the "Kingdom of Heaven" is personally present. For Christians, this Kingdom is, therefore, a present reality as well as a divine condition and future promise.

LEADERSHIP: Leadership is the art of moving a group toward a preferred objective. In this book, the terms "leader" and "shepherd" are used interchangeably, in order to emphasize the Biblical metaphor of leaders as servants and shepherds of those under their care, dedicated to the best interests of followers. Leadership is a complex phenomenon involving both leaders and followers within a specific cultural context. Nevertheless, this book suggests that underlying all true leadership, there is an element of service to the greater good.

NON ACTION: One of the most puzzling parts of the *Tao Te Ching* is the use of the term, "non-action" *(Wu-Wei)*. To the Western mind, this either has the connotation of passivity in the face of problems or evil, or of pacifism in the face of conflict. Thus, some scholars and writers have a hard time coordinating the military advice of Lao Tzu with this principle of inactivity. Properly understood, the principle involves not so much inactivity, as not acting beyond what is required. The principle is one of restraint, patience, and prudence in action.

ONE WHO IS: It is difficult to maintain the "feel" of the *Tao Te Ching* while paraphrasing it with a Christian flavor. In this work, various terms are used for God, the most frequent of which is the "One Who Is." This is a reference taken from Exodus, where God refers to himself as "I Am," using a Hebrew term translated as "I Am that I Am" or "I Will Be What I Will Be" (See Exodus 3:14). I have referred to God as "One Who Is and Will Be" to capture God's inscrutable sovereignty over the future as well as the present. See definition of "Eternal".

PEACE: Peace, like the Hebrew term "Shalom," is not merely the absence of conflict, but a state where all things are properly ordered.

Peace is a condition of relational wholeness. It is a state where creation and persons are property aligned so that the needs of all things and all people are met.

SIMPLICITY: The term "Uncarved Block" refers to a state of natural simplicity. Lao Tzu uses the term "Uncarved Block" *(Pu)* to refer to the life of simplicity, frugality, humility, and deep love. One attains this kind of simplicity when one lives without hypocrisy or artificiality and without a need for an overabundance of physical possessions or social attainments.

TAO: This term, often translated as "Way" defies complete translation. Sometimes, it is used as a way of referring to the ultimate nature of reality, "the Way Things Are." In this metaphysical sense, it refers to ultimate uncreated cause from which reality emerges. It is also the underlying rationality and reason by which all things were created. This usage is close to the meaning of the Greek term "Logos." At other times, "Tao" is used to describe the kind of life a wise person chooses to live. In this usage "Tao" has a moral connotation. This usage is close to the use of the terms "Path," "Road," or "Way" in Judeo-Christian wisdom literature.

VIRTUE: This term is a translation of the Chinese term, *Te.* Te refers to the innate power of the moral characteristics of those who follow the Way. This kind of character is created by meditation upon and embodiment of the Word as one follows the Way of Christ, the virtuous power of the life lived according to the Way of Christ.

WORD: This term, used in the first chapter of John to describe the pre-incarnate Christ, refers to the first principle of existence, the LOGOS, the Divine Ground of rationality and reason in the created order. It is this Divine Rationality, or principle of rationality, that stands beneath and supports all created rationality. In John the term "Word" (*Logos*) refers to the Second Person of the Trinity. In Christ, the uncreated rationality and reason of God, through which he created the world, took on human form and became visible within the confines of the created order. (See John 1:1).

WAY: In Wisdom literature, the term "Way" is used to describe the character of the life of the wise person and the fool. The fool walks in the way (path or road) of a fool, and the wise person walks in the way (path or road) of wisdom. In this sense, the word "Way" has a practical, ethical connotation. The wise person is that well-adjusted individual who is able to successfully walk according to the ethical and practical demands of life. The term "Way" describes way of life and character patterned after the example of the Word revealed in Christ as testified to by the Gospels. This is the true path to personal and relational wholeness.

YIN/YANG: This term is used to describe the male and female principles of the universe and also refers to the dualities of light and dark, action and inaction, and the like. In the Tao, wisdom is often found in embracing the female or the passive aspect of the human personality. Since Christianity has no metaphysical categories that coordinate with Yin and Yang, I have normally paraphrased using concepts such as "activity" and "inactivity." In this adaptation, what the Tao refers to as the "female," I have phrased in terms of receptivity. I have often used the terms Light and Love to refer to the duality between relationality and truthfulness, which finds complete unity in the Eternal God. In a similar way, the Tao uses the male and female to refer to the duality that exists within all of us to embrace both doing and being, and acting and waiting.

BIBLIOGRAPHY

Books Related to the *Tao Te Ching*

Martin Aronson, *Jesus and the Tao: Parallel Sayings with Commentary* (Berkeley, CA: Seastone, 2000).

Heromonk Damascene, *Christ the Eternal Tao* (Platina, CA: Valaam, 1999).

Lao Tzu, *Tao Te Ching* tr. Derek Lin (Woodstock VT: Skylight Paths Publishing, 2006).

Lao Tzu, *The Tao Te Ching of Lao Tzu* tr. Brian Brown Walker (New York, NY: St. Martin's Press, 1995) Chapter 51.

Lao Tzu, *Tao Te Ching: A New English Version* tr. Stephen Mitchell (New York, NY: Harper & Row, 1988).

Lao Tzu, *Tao Te Ching: A New Translation* B. Wai-Tao and D. Goddard, tr. 2nd ed. (Santa Barbra, CA: Dwight Goddard, 1935).

Lao Tzu, *Tao Te Ching*. tr. D. G. Lau (Middlesex, England, UK: Penguin, 1963).

Lao Tzu, *Tao Te Ching* tr. Gia Fu-Feng & Jane English. int. Jacob Needleman (New York, NY: Vintage Books, 1989).

Lao Tzu, *The Tao of Power: Lao Tzu's Classic Guide to Leadership, Influence and Excellence* tr. R. L. Wing (Garden City: Doubleday, 1986).

Lao Tzu, *Tao Te Ching - A Translation For the Public Domain* tr. J. H. McDonald www.Wright-house.com/religions/taoism (1996).

William C. Martin, *The Art of Pastoring: Contemplative Reflections* (Decatur. GA: CTS Press, 1994).

Wing-Tsit Chan, *The Way of Lao Tzu (Tao-te Ching)* tr. Wing-Tsit Chan (New York: Macmillian, 1963).

Joseph A. Loya, Wan Li Ho, Chang-Sin Jih, *The Tao of Jesus* (New York: Paulist Press, 1998).

Alan Watts, "What is the Tao?" in *Eastern Wisdom: Three Classics in One Volume* (New York, NY: MJf Books, 2001).

Bible Translations

Contemporary English Version (New York, NY: American Bible Society, 1995) (CEV).

New Revised Standard Version Bible (New York, NY: Division of Christian Education of the National Council of Churches of Christ, 1989) (NRSV)

The New International Version (Colorado Springs, CO: International Bible Society, 1984) (NIV).

English Standard Version (Wheaton, Ill: Crossway Publishers, 2005-2009) (ESV).

New Century Version (Dallas, TX: Word Publishing, 1991) (NCV).

New Living Translation (Wheaton, Ill: Tyndale House Publishers, 1996) (NLT).

New King James Version (Nashville, TN: Thomas Nelson, 1980) (NKJV).

Today's English Version (New York, NY: American Bible Society, 1976) (TEV).

Today's New International Version (Colorado Springs, CO: International Bible Society 2001, 2005 (TNIV).

Revised English Bible with the Apocrypha (Oxford & Cambridge, England Oxford University Press & Cambridge University Press, 1989) (REV)

Revised Standard Version (New York: National Council of Churches, 1952) (RSV).

Eugene H. Peterson, *The Message: The Bible in Contemporary Language* (Colorado Springs, CO: NavPress, 2003) (Message).

J. B. Phillips, *The New Testament in Modern Language* (New York, NY: The Mamillan Company, 1958) (Phillips).

Each version of the Holy Bible quoted in this work is used within the copyright restrictions of the publisher.

Each publisher reserves all rights to their work pursuant to applicable copyright laws.

<u>Other Works of Interest</u>

James A. Autry, *The Servant Leader: How to Build a Creative Team, Develop Great Morale, and Improve Bottom Line Performance* (Roseville, CA: Prima Publishing, 2001).

James A. Autrey & Stephen Mitchell, *Real Power: Business Lessons from the Tao Te Ching* (New York, NY: Riverhead Books, 1998).

John Beverly Butcher, *The Tao of Jesus: A Book of Days for the Natural Year* rev. ed. (Berkeley, CA: Apocryphile Press, 1994).

Robert K, Greenleaf, *Servant Leadership: A Journey into the Nature of Legitimate Power and Greatness* (New York, NY: Paulist Press, 1977).

John Heider, *The Tao of Leadership: Lao Tzu's Tao Te Ching Adapted for a New Age* (Atlanta, GA: Humanics, 1985).

C. S. Lewis, *The Abolition of Man* (New York, NY: Collier Books, 1947).

Bennett J. Sims, *Servanthood: Leadership for the Third Millennium* (Boston, MA: Crowley Publications, 1997).

Made in the USA
Charleston, SC
26 June 2010